asked to officiate

AMERICAN MARRIAGE MINISTRIES
ASKED TO OFFICIATE

COPYRIGHT © 2018 BY AMERICAN MARRIAGE MINISTRIES

ALL RIGHTS RESERVED. IN ACCORDANCE WITH THE US COPYRIGHT ACT OF 1976, THE SCANNING, UPLOADING, AND ELECTRONIC SHARING OF ANY PART OF THIS BOOK WITHOUT THE PERMISSION OF THE PUBLISHER IS UNLAWFUL PIRACY AND THEFT OF THE AUTHORS INTELLECTUAL PROPERTY. IF YOU WOULD LIKE TO USE MATERIAL FROM THE BOOK, PRIOR WRITTEN PERMISSION MUST BE OBTAINED BY CONTACTING THE PUBLISHER AT INFO@THEAMM.ORG. THANK YOU FOR YOUR SUPPORT OF THE AUTHOR'S RIGHTS.

AMERICAN MARRIAGE MINISTRIES
304 ALASKAN WAY S STE 102
SEATTLE, WA 98104

WWW.THEAMM.ORG

PRINTED IN THE UNITED STATES OF AMERICA

CURRENT EDITION: MAY 2021

The 2018 Edition of Asked to Officiate features rewrites and other contributions by American Marriage Ministries staff including Natasha Anakotta, Dylan Wall, Lewis King, and Gregory Flores. American Marriage Ministries would also like to thank Bethel Nathan and the thousands of other AMM Ministers who have helped make this book possible.

asked to officiate

your complete guide to a perfect ceremony

Step by Step Workbook

by American Marriage Ministries and
Bethel Nathan of Ceremonies by Bethel

asked to officiate table of contents

- 1   **Introduction**
- 3   **Get Ordained!**
- 7   **LGBTQ couples**
- 13   **Planning With the Couple**
- 17   **Ceremony Creation**
  - an introduction 17
  - the parent's blessing 21
  - opening remarks 25
  - religious & spiritual words 29
  - family & guest's blessings and rememberance . . 35
  - words on marriage 41
  - the couple's story 51
  - vows 57
  - the ring ceremony 77
  - readings 83
  - traditions & rituals 91
  - closing remarks 101
  - pronouncement, kiss, and introduction 105
  - ceremony assembly 111
- 113   **Preparation for Ceremony Delivery**
- 117   **Rehearsing the Ceremony**
- 125   **Directing the Ceremony**
- 133   **Delivering the Ceremony**
- 135   **Glossary**

1 Introduction

Welcome to *Asked to Officiate*!

This book is for everyone planning, administering, or simply celebrating the perfect wedding. Whether you are a partner writing your vows or planning the wedding, an officiant preparing the ceremony, or one of the many other organizers that make weddings so special, this book is for you.

American Marriage Ministries (AMM) has ordained more than 512,544 ministers around the world. That translates into millions of weddings that AMM Ministers have performed, tens-of-millions of hours of experience, and quite possibly the most diverse group of officiants in the world. No matter what sort of wedding you want to perform, we can help.

With decades of collective experience organizing and officiating weddings, we at AMM understand the tremendous pressure and expectations that have been placed on you. *Asked to Officiate* empowers you to make this ceremony authentic, meaningful, and memorable, and we're here to help you every step of the way.

AMM's story is part of a broader change in the way that people approach important life events such as marriage. We're learning that meaning in life comes from listening to our inner voices and choosing authenticity over conformity. Choosing to marry someone is one of the most important decisions we make in our lives, and we want our ceremonies to reflect that. When we get married, we are welcoming our partners into our families and communities, and we want the people around us to be involved in the process. It's common place now for couples to ask a friend or family member to officiate their ceremony. That's a big responsibility, and for many of us, it might be the first time.

You're probably nervous. You're wondering what to say. You might have reservations about public speaking. It's a big event and you want to do the best job possible. Stop, and take a deep breath, because you are already holding a copy of *Asked to Officiate*. We'll get through this together. Everything is going to work out just fine!

This book is your end-to-end guide to the ceremony preparation and presentation process. Our goal is to take the stress and complication out of the process, allowing you to experience the joy and wonder of the wedding.

When you started looking into performing a wedding, one of the first things that you probably heard was, "you can get ordained online." And while that is absolutely true, there is so much more to officiating a wedding than simply being legally permitted to sign a marriage license. The wedding ceremony is the most important part of every couple's special day, and we want to help you shine in this moment of honor and responsibility.

Asked to Officiate cuts through the information overload of an online search. Our step-by-step instructions cover the four pillars of the wedding ceremony, letting you plan at your own pace, to your own specifications, exactly as you see fit.

the four components

1. **Legal** What do I need to know to legally officiate a wedding?
2. **Preparation** How do I create a meaningful ceremony?
3. **The Ceremony** How do I conduct the ceremony in a professional and impactful way?
4. **Logistics** What is my role as a ceremony director, and how do I sign the marriage license.

We've broken down the how-to for each of these components. All you need to do now is work your way through the chapters and apply our suggestions to the specifics of your wedding. Good Luck!

2 Get Ordained!

You've been asked to officiate a friend or family member's wedding, so what's next? The first order of business is making sure that you have the legal authority to perform marriages. Once you are ordained with American Marriage Ministries, you can check that box.

In most states, there's no additional registration required, but some states, territories, counties, and even some towns require a few extra steps before you can legally officiate. It's important to get the paperwork out of the way early so you can concentrate on what really matters - the ceremony!

Finding out what you need to do next is as easy as entering your state on our website. It only takes a few seconds to find out everything you need to know at: *theamm.org/minister-registration*

establishing your legal right to perform weddings

There's a reason everyone hates visiting the DMV — bureaucracy is tiresome, forms are tedious, and your time is precious. But if you follow the advice in this chapter, taking care of any paperwork with your local government shouldn't take long, and the process should be relatively painless. To make it even easier, use the following three-step process:

1. **Go online and get ordained**
   Start out by entering theamm.org into your browser and get ordained.

2. **Check out the local laws and make sure you are in compliance**
   Use AMM's Legal Requirements tool on our website to find out about regulations in your state, and follow registration steps if necessary.

3. **Perform the marriage!**
   Ordination through theamm.org confers full legal religious authority upon our ministers. Once you're ordained and registered, you're good to go.

In most states, once you are ordained as a minister with a church like American Marriage Ministries, you have the right to perform marriage and sign a marriage license. However, some states require additional registration, and some provide options for non-ministers, but as an AMM Minister, your credentials will be recognized throughout the United States.

AMM believes...

A couple's marriage ceremony is also a deeply personal expression of their values and beliefs. As an officiant, choosing where to become ordained should reflect those principles.

An ordination from American Marriage Ministries is an affirmation of your beliefs. No prior ministerial experience is necessary to officiate. Ordination is free and does not expire. No matter what your religion, gender, or background, we want you to advance this remarkable institution. We embrace your's and the couple's diversity, history, and ambitions as you choose your paths in life.

That brings us to the three pillars of our belief:

i. **All people, regardless of race, gender, or sexual orientation, have the right to marry.**

ii. **It is the right of every couple to choose who will solemnize their marriage.**

iii. **All people have the right to solemnize marriage.**

Marriage is a right, a freedom, and a social guarantee that underpins the society in which we live. As you set out to officiate, American Marriage Ministries is your ally.

Guided by these principals, we have spent years establishing the most comprehensive legal standing and representation possible. Our lawyers and researchers have worked tirelessly to protect our minster's legal right to perform marriages and we have incorporated their findings into the most user-friendly online ordination platform available.

In addition to full legal standing, our ordained ministers can perform their duties backed by the spotless reputation of American Marriage Ministries. Since our founding on July 4, 2009, we have advanced a non-partisan progressive agenda of equal rights and mutual respect for our fellow citizens. Now, we invite you to join us for the next chapter, bringing together friends, family, community, and celebrating love across this great nation.

3 LGBTQ Couples

LGBTQ weddings are increasingly common, but since that wasn't always the case, LGBTQ couples don't have centuries of marriage tradition to fall back on in the way that heterosexual couples do. While that might seem like a challenge, it's also a great opportunity for the couple to express themselves without the pressure to conform.

That said, there are some nuances to be aware of. While marriage equality is now a national movement, the LGBTQ struggle for equality is far from over. For many, in addition to a statement of love and commitment, a wedding is a personal or political statement that factors into the ceremony and the planning. Throughout the book, we have added comments or suggestions pertaining to LGBTQ couples, wherever they are relevant, to help our readers adapt any ceremony as needed.

pronouns and gendered language

In the interest of being as inclusive as possible, *Asked to Officiate* avoids using gender in most instances, but ultimately, it's the couple's wedding, and that means using whatever language they are comfortable with.

In keeping with our belief that all people are entitled to enter into marriage, we have avoided gendered pronouns such as "Husband" and "Wife" wherever possible, instead using "Partner 1" and "Partner 2." However, when it comes to planning traditional ceremonies for "Brides" and "Grooms," we've occasionally retained those designations, because some couples might want an old fashioned wedding. Our goal is to assist you, no matter what your orientation or beliefs.

creating a ceremony that fits

We've learned that there's no one-size-fits-all approach to ceremonies. With that in mind, what matters most is that the ceremony reflects the couple's relationship, and honors who they are together using words that speak to them. As you begin planning the ceremony, it's helpful to explore some traditional components of a marriage ceremony, adapting them as necessary to create your own version.

the procession

There is no shortage of ways to walk down the aisle, but here are some common versions to consider:

- One partner waits up at the front with the officiant, while the other partner walks in with his/her escort.

- One partner walks in with his/her escort, and then the other follows with his/her escort.

- Both partners walk in together.

Now you can start mixing it up! Some couples opt for two aisles instead of the traditional single aisle. If the venue accommodates this setup, it gives you a lot of options. Plus, just like flying, more aisle seats mean better visibility and mobility. The two-aisle setup, allows partners to enter together from the back of the assembly, walk down their respective aisles, and meet at the front, together as equals. It also accommodates more traditional entrances.

In a LGBTQ wedding, partners don't always identify as "Brides" or "Grooms." As a result, they may not want to perform traditional bride and groom roles during the ceremony. Many LGBTQ couples who are marrying have already been together for a long time. A ceremony that allows them to enter separately and meet in the middle is a powerful symbol of their unity.

the pronouncement

The pronouncement traditionally included the phrase, "…I now pronounce you husband and wife." We're rethinking that now, making this an opportunity to replace the standard phrasing with words that speak to the couple. Make sure to discuss what words express their identity, and what terms they plan to use to describe themselves once they are married.

Some couples want to use "partners for life" or "spouses for life." Others want to emphasize the legal significance of their marriage, using "legal partners in life" or something to that effect. Others want to hear the traditional (and sometimes powerful) words of "husband and husband" or "wife and wife." You can even combine options. For example, the officiant can say, "I pronounce you husbands/wives, spouses, and legal partners in life!" These words are a recognition of a long history and struggle for equality, and its important to give them due consideration.

the kiss and presentation

The first married kiss is another part of the wedding ceremony that has immense significance and a long history that needs to be taken into consideration. With the right forethought, the first married kiss provides that picture-perfect wedding moment. In the *Pronouncement, Kiss, and Presentation* section of the *Ceremony Creation* chapter (page 105), there are a variety of choices, all of which can be adapted to accommodate LGBTQ couples. Some partners enjoy thinking of themselves as a bride or a groom, while others find those words don't fit them. And some may want to emphasize that there are two, using phrases such as, "you may now each kiss your bride!"

the foundation covenant

One popular addition to the ceremony, created by LGBTQ wedding planner Bernadette Smith for her own wedding, is the signing of a *Foundation Covenant* by the couple and wedding attendees. This ceremony invites the active participation of wedding guests and is a powerful statement of community and purpose.

Here's how it works. After the vows are exchanged, the wedding officiant asks the couple to sign the Foundation Covenant, an artistically inspired wedding document that draws on Jewish and Quaker traditions. Immediately following the ceremony, the Foundation Covenant is displayed in a place where family, friends, and other attendees can sign it, affirming their support for the newly married couple.

readings

Some couples use their wedding ceremony as an opportunity to make a political statement about marriage equality. There is a rich canon of material out there that couples can choose from, drawing on the writings of early

LGBTQ activists and allies. Other couples have chosen to read aloud excerpts from important court cases that substantiated marriage equality. After millennia of discrimination, these legal victories are important steps in the struggle for LGBTQ equality. For many, these pro-marriage equality verdicts vindicate years of struggle. The fight is far from over, however, and every LGBTQ wedding is a public statement that all people are created equal.

examples

Justice Kennedy in the Marriage Equality Supreme Court decision, June 26, 2015
No union is more profound than marriage, for it embodies the highest ideals of love, fidelity, devotion, sacrifice, and family. In forming a marital union, two people become something greater than once they were.

Goodridge v. Department of Health by Massachusetts Supreme Court Chief Justice Margaret H. Marshall
"Marriage is a vital social institution. The exclusive commitment of two individuals to each other nurtures love and mutual support; it brings stability to our society. For those who choose to marry, and for their children, marriage provides an abundance of legal, financial, and social benefits. In return it imposes weighty legal, financial, and social obligations. ...

Without question, civil marriage enhances the "welfare of the community." It is a "social institution of the highest importance." ...

Marriage also bestows enormous private and social advantages on those who choose to marry. Civil marriage is at once a deeply personal commitment to another human being and a highly public celebration of the ideals of mutuality, companionship, intimacy, fidelity, and family. ...

Because it fulfills yearnings for security, safe haven, and connection that express our common humanity, civil marriage is an esteemed institution, and the decision whether and whom to marry is among life's momentous acts of self-definition."

Excerpts from Prop 8 Ruling by Judge Vaughn Walker
"Marriage is the state recognition and approval of a couple's choice to live with each other, to remain committed to one another and to form a household based on their own feelings about one another and to join in an economic partnership and support one another and any dependents…"

"The right to marry has been historically and remains the right to choose a spouse and, with mutual consent, join together and form a household. Race and gender restrictions shaped marriage during eras of race and gender inequality, but such restrictions were never part of the historical core of the institution of marriage. Today, gender is not relevant to the state in determining spouses' obligations to each other and to their dependents. Relative gender composition aside, same-sex couples are situated identically to opposite-sex couples in terms of their ability to perform the rights and obligations of marriage under California law. Gender no longer forms an essential part of marriage; marriage under law is a union of equals…"

"They seek the mutual obligation and honor that attend marriage… seek recognition from the state that their union is 'a coming together for better or for worse, hopefully enduring, and intimate to the degree of being sacred.'"

4 Planning With the Couple

Marriage ceremonies are all about chemistry, chemistry is about bonding, and bonding is about putting in the time and effort. That's why meeting with the couple to discuss the ceremony is one of the most important preparations in the lead up to the wedding. In addition to establishing a clear, unified vision for the ceremony, this meeting is a chance for you to get to know each other. If you already know the couple well, all the better, but make sure you take the time to build an open and honest rapport that allows you to create a meaningful ceremony.

getting on the same page

In addition to learning about each other, planning with the couple should include a step-by-step preview of the ceremony to establish your roles and what's expected of you. Don't leave anything to chance.

In order to make the meeting as productive as possible, we recommend that everyone involved in the ceremony reviews this book. Doing your homework will ensure that everyone arrives at the meeting with clearly defined expectations and is ready to get to work.

who's writing the ceremony?

The Couple
Even if the couple are writing the ceremony and they have a detailed plan in place, taking the time to meet helps you, their officiant, understand and execute the ceremony. It may seem straightforward to the couple, but it never hurts to review. You still need to discuss what tone and style of delivery is expected of you.

Sharing your expectations for the ceremony helps avoid unpleasant surprises later on. There might be religious passages or embarrassing stories in the script that make someone uncomfortable. In a worst case scenario, the couple still has plenty of time to find another officiant if you aren't a good match.

The Officiant
If you are involved in writing the ceremony, planning with the couple is your chance to determine what the couple has in mind, and explore different options for the ceremony. Using this book, both couple and officiant can piece together a personalized ceremony from the options provided.

the consultation

By following our step-by-step approach, you can create the desired atmosphere and feel for the ceremony. It's important that everyone is on the same page. You don't want to find out at the last minute that the couple want to stage a supernatural wedding – which is fine as long as everyone is in agreement – and that the officiant is expected to hide behind a curtain and use his or her *Wizard of Oz* voice.

Remember that this celebration isn't about the officiant or the officiant's preferences. Weddings are a celebration of the couple, and your role as an officiant is to enable that during the ceremony. For some officiants, there might be the temptation to fall back on comedy, but in almost all instances, those sorts of routines are best saved for the reception, rather than the wedding ceremony.

questions for the couple

In the next section, we have provided some questions that have helped our ministers understand their couple's expectations and wishes. Bring a notebook and jot down your observations! As always, these questions are just guidelines, so feel free to expand on these questions as you see fit.

1. How long should the ceremony be?
In our opinion, the sweet spot is between 15 and 20 minutes. That's enough time for a personal and meaningful ceremony (some laughs and some tears). If the ceremony runs too long, your guests will start checking their watches and casting longing glances towards the bar.

2. What does the couple want to include in their ceremony, and what do they want to avoid?
A great strategy for this question is to encourage a stream of consciousness. Ask the couple to express any and all expectations they might have about the feel they want to create and content that appeals to their imagination. If you encounter blank stares or shrugs, ask the couple if there are any poems they want to incorporate, traditions that can be woven into the ceremony (e.g. breaking of the glass), or other rituals they might want to explore.

Don't hesitate to ask clarifying questions. Phrases like, "spiritual, but not religious" mean different things to different people.

Ultimately, it's the couple's ceremony; the officiant is the facilitator. Since most AMM Ministers conduct weddings outside of traditional places of worship – most mainstream churches only accept clergy of their particular denomination – there are few rules you have to comply with. If the couple need inspiration, help them explore their common history and shared passions.

Beyond filing a marriage license with the local government, the only ceremony requirement is the declaration of intent (the "I do" part). Everything else is up to the couple. For traditional couples, lines such as, "you may now kiss the bride," are the perfect conclusion to the ceremony. Others want to avoid anything that might be heard on a television show or in a movie. There's no right or wrong answer; it's up to the couple!

3. Are there family expectations that should be factored in?
Whether it's a poem that grandma reads at every family ceremony, a sacred text from mom, or a cousin that's going to play trumpet as the couple walk in, you want to know what's going to happen. Not only will that preempt unexpected surprises, it will also allow you to design or modify the ceremony to complement those contributions.

4. How many, and what sort of guests will be in attendance?

It's always important to "know your audience," and this is especially the case with weddings. Will most of the attendees be close family? Will the couple be inviting dozens of their college friends and coworkers? Are they religious folk? These details matter when you are planning the ceremony, and getting clear answers will help you determine the best messaging and tone.

the next steps

After you have covered these questions, it's time to establish who is responsible for what, and set clear deadlines. Get that ceremony written, figure out what those readings are going to be, and make a plan to check back in. While this might sound like a term paper or a work assignment, everyone has a vested interest in making the ceremony go smoothly. And unlike office projects, weddings are much more interesting and fun!

 By now, it should be clear that officiating a wedding entails a lot more than just reading words from a notebook.

As the officiant, you need to ask yourself, are you up to the task? It's much better to realize early on that you are not suited for the role, and to pass it on to someone else. Most professional officiants and planners can recount stories of panicked calls just days before the wedding from couples scrambling to replace a friend or family member that got cold feet. Remember, there's nothing wrong with deferring to someone else as long as you give the couple time to make alternate plans.

5.1 Ceremony Creation
an introduction

While there is no "legally correct," way to conduct a wedding ceremony - beyond some states requiring an "I do" - most ceremonies follow recognizable cultural conventions, and there's a reason for that. Weddings are a public expression of the couple's sacred bond, and the most effective way to communicate is through easily recognizable and shared symbols.

As the officiant, your role is to help the couple decide how and what they want to express through their ceremony. Your active participation in the lead-up to the event ensures that the wedding ceremony goes smoothly.

the step-by-step approach:

It's time to start putting the ceremony together! To make the process easier, we have broken the ceremony down into its different components, with each section of this chapter covering a particular part of the ceremony. All you have to do is pick the parts you want, make them your own, and assemble them into a complete ceremony.

 Speaking of picking and assembling, you'll probably want to jot down notes as you work your way through this chapter. Whether you're keeping tabs on your phone or writing in a notebook, it's important to stay organized. Doing so make it easy to go from reading this book to planning the ceremony. You may even want to revisit your notes to write the wedding program.

We have provided helpful tips and a selection of prewritten options which can be used in your ceremony. If you're looking for even more examples and inspiration, head on over to the AMM website.

As always, this book is a guide, not a set of rules. If something in these pages inspires you, don't hesitate to modify it to suit the couple's wishes. It's fine to "color outside the lines," as long as the ceremony flows well.

Ceremony Creation an introduction | 17

ceremony sections covered in this book:

The Parent's Blessing 21
Opening Remarks 25
Religious & Spiritual Words 29
Family & Guest's Blessings and Rememberance 35
Words on Marriage 41
The Couple's Story 51
Vows 57
The Ring Ceremony 77
Readings 83
Traditions & Rituals 91
Closing Remarks 101
The Pronouncement, Kiss, and Introduction 105
Ceremony Assembly 111

While there are quite a few parts that make up a traditional wedding ceremony, you don't want it to run more than 20 minutes, which means making sure no one piece runs too long. Remember, not all pieces need to be used.

If this is all getting a bit overwhelming, don't worry. As you progress through this part of the book, we provide plenty of pre-written options for each ceremony piece that you can use or adapt. By the end of this chapter, you'll be well on your way to completion.

a quick reminder

You are trying to keep the same overall tone throughout the ceremony. While there might be tears one minute, and laughter the next, the emphasis on love and commitment should be consistent.

Other than the five fundamental pieces below, in the order shown, the rest of the ceremony structure is flexible. If, for example, you want to move the family blessing toward the end, go for it!

The 5 Critical Components
1. Opening Remarks
2. Vows
3. Ring Exchange
4. Closing Words
5. The Pronouncement, Kiss, and Introduction

5.2 Ceremony Creation
the parent's blessing

The Parent's Blessing - sometimes referred to as the 'end-of-aisle' question or traditionally the 'giving of the bride' - is posed to the father, mother, both parents, or another escort(s), after the bride has walked down the aisle. Couples can choose between modern, traditional, or alternative style questions, or they can forgo the question altogether.

This tradition is grounded in the historical practice of the bride's father "giving" her away. Because this practice is associated with an era when many women were deprived of a choice in the matter, many modern brides avoid this part of the ceremony, or adapt it to reflect their emancipated status.

> **in practice...**
> *Aida had no intention of being "given away" to anyone. Her parents on the other hand, were more traditional, and she knew they would want to give some sort of blessing. Sure they weren't handing her off in the conventional sense, but to Aida's mother, there was a bittersweet component. It felt like she was "losing her baby girl." Aida's partner Sven was just as uncomfortable with the idea of being on the receiving end of such a ceremony. After discussing it with their officiant, they decided on a wording that acknowledged her parent's years of love and sacrifice, without sounding patriarchal.*

other ways to acknowledge parents and family

Aida and Sven's choice reflected *their* values, but each couple is different. Deciding whether to include the Parent's Blessing is a personal choice. While this part of the ceremony is an opportunity to celebrate the bond between a parent and child, some couples will want to drop it for personal reasons. Either way, we recommend that you approach this option with sensitivity.

If the couple decides to include a *Family Blessing* (page 35), especially one where the families are asked for their blessings and support, including this piece in the ceremony may feel redundant.

incorporating the blessing

If the Middle Ground option (below) is chosen, we recommend that it be included during the *Opening Remarks* (page 25). The questions fits nicely between the two paragraphs of the opening remarks.

The Parent's Blessing should only last a few seconds, and is incorporated into the final few feet of the bride's walk down the aisle with her escort.

At this point in the planning process, you only need to decide whether you want to include this in your ceremony, and if so, which variation. Later, in *Directing the Ceremony* (page 125), we explain how to choreograph the blessing.

examples

Modern

Minister: Who supports _____ as she and _____ take
                              Partner 1   Partner 2
this next step together?
Family: Her mother and I do.

Traditional

Minister: Who presents this woman in marriage?
Family: Her mother and I do.

Middle Ground, Styled in Celtic Tradition

Minister: Marriage is a bond to be entered into only after considerable thought and reflection. As with any aspect of life, it has its cycles, its ups and its downs, its trials and its triumphs. With full understanding of this, _____ and
                                                                                                                                            Bride

_____ have come here today to be joined as one in marriage. Others
   Groom
would ask, at this time, 'who gives the bride in marriage,' but, as a woman is not property to be bought and sold, given and taken, I ask simply if she comes of her own will and if she has her family's blessing. _____ is it true that you come
                                                                Bride
of your own free will and accord?

Bride: Yes, it is.

Minister: Does she come with her family's blessing?

Family: Yes, she does.

5.3 Ceremony Creation
opening remarks

The opening remarks announce the formal beginning of the ceremony, and are the time for an introductory and welcoming message. The couple have arrived at the front of the room, the guests are seated, and it's time to marry the couple. You don't want to keep them standing there too long.

> **in practice...**
> Cathy and Zach knew that many of their guests had traveled a long way to witness their wedding day. A study by The Knot found that wedding guests spent an average of $888 when traveling to attend weddings, and for attendants, that figure increased to an average of $1,154 per wedding. Cathy and Zach used the opening remarks to acknowledge the sacrifices their friends and family had made to be there and how much it meant to them.

In two paragraphs, set the tone for the ceremony, welcome everyone, and tell them why they are in attendance – to witness the couple's marriage, of course. You'll have some leeway to dispense advice or comment on the importance of marriage and commitment, but the focus must be on welcoming the guests, the ceremony, and most importantly, the couple.

examples

> **Guests from Near and Far**
>
> Welcome to the family and friends who traveled from near and far to be here today. I know that your presence means the world to _____ (Partner 1) and _____ (Partner 2). We are all honored to be a part of their public pronouncement of their love and commitment to each other.
>
> Some of you may have been participants in their relationship in the beginning, as their love took shape and blossomed. Others here got to know them later, as they grew from two people who were "just dating" into a couple. To some of you, they

have always been the wonderful couple that we witness standing before us today. But regardless of how _____ (Partner 1) and _____ (Partner 2) came into our lives, we are all honored to be here for the most important time in their relationship… the public declaration of their love and commitment to each other.

Joyous Occasion

All of us gathered here today, family and friends of this wonderful couple, have come together to celebrate a most joyous occasion. All of us are fortunate to have been asked to witness the most important transition in a relationship between two people. This is the transition in which two people in love commit themselves to each other, in word and action.

They take this step not because they need to, but because they want to. They desire to publicly pledge their love for each other, and commitment to each other. _____ (Partner 1) and _____ (Partner 2) we are honored to bear witness to this transition and we know that you are not taking this step lightly. Many here have watched as your love for each other has grown and matured from the awkwardness of that first date, into the perfection that you manifest today. Today, we are privileged witnesses to this important step, as you proclaim you love for all the world to see.

Merging of Communities

A warmest welcome to you all — family and friends, those who care about this couple, and have come from near and far to celebrate with them. _____ (Partner 1) and _____ (Partner 2) have asked us to be a part of this celebration of their love for each other, and it is with great joy and reverence that we all take part. They seek to continue the commitment, which of course does not begin today, but which began in wonder some time ago when they found love in each other. There are many stages and kinds of commitment, but this one is the deepest, the most sacred. It is a love that comes out of the clear choice of two people.

With this step, the couple is merging their individual lives, their families and friends, joining themselves and their communities into one that is bigger and more powerful. Their love has prevailed by virtue of its strengths. Yet marriage adds a new dimension, which they approach with enthusiasm and deepening love. Our hearts are filled with happiness on this special day. It has been said that marriage is falling in love over and over again with the same person. How _____ (Partner 1) and _____ (Partner 2) will continue to accomplish this will be up to them, for every marriage is as unique as the people that it joins. What we do know, however, is that they have found much to share and much to enrich their lives together.

★★★

Tastefully Casual

I'd like to welcome the family, the friends, and most importantly, the couple, _____ (Partner 1) and _____ (Partner 2). Each and every one of us is honored to be here celebrating this incredibly joyous occasion, witnessing the most important day in their lives together. As _____ (Partner 1) and _____ (Partner 2) take their relationship to the next level, this gathering is a testament to love and solidarity.

Some might say that _____ (Partner 1) and _____ (Partner 2) are already committed to each other, and I wouldn't disagree. But today, they are proclaiming that commitment not only to us, the people closest to them, but to the world as well. They are saying, "we love each other, we support each other, and we want to spend the rest of our lives together."

★★★

Honoring Marriage

Friends and family, join me in welcoming _____ (Partner 1) and _____ (Partner 2)! And _____ (Partner 1) and _____ (Partner 2), I know that I speak for everyone when I say that we are honored to be here to celebrate this most important day with the two of you. This is the day when you publicly declare your love for, and commitment to, each other. This is the day when the bond between you will be sealed in word and action… and witnessed by those you hold most dear.

Without context, marriage is just a word. It's the love that you have for each other that gives the word its power. It's the promises that you are about to make to each other that give marriage its significance. It's the unity of your bond that stands as a testament to the world, affirming that you, _____ share the deepest and most sacred love.
_{Partner 1 & Partner 2}

5.4 Ceremony Creation
religious & spiritual words

This is where you would quote from the Bible, read from the Torah, recite verses from the Quran, or give expression to any other religious and spiritual beliefs that the couple or their families might hold. For many couples, their ceremony is an extension of their spiritual lives, and readings are an effective way to communicate their beliefs.

A couple's religious and spiritual convictions are profoundly personal, which is precisely why so many couples ask a friend or family member to officiate their wedding. There's a good chance that's why you are reading this book right now! And since weddings should reflect the couple's beliefs, the officiant needs to be sensitive to these matters and help the couple express their spirituality through the ceremony.

finding the right balance

Every couple is different, and navigating religion and spirituality requires a certain finesse. While some couples might not want their ceremony to be "religious," they will still include such language to make their religiously-inclined family members feel included and welcomed.

> **in practice...**
> *Steve wasn't particularly religious but his partner Devin always attended church on high holidays, and came from a religious family. Left to Devin, their wedding would have featured a priest in robes and sacred hymns. Ultimately both were more concerned about each other's happiness, so they compromised with a short reading that spoke to Devin's spirituality without bothering Steve.*
>
> *Steve and Devin went with a short, but meaningful option that communicated to their religious guests that the couple took their guests' beliefs seriously, without being overtly religious.*

There are subtle ways to account for guests' religious beliefs without compromising the couple's own principles. The key here is to find the middle ground and define the couple's comfort zone. There's a difference between proselytizing and quoting a religious passage that conveys the importance of the moment.

If certain religious language or rituals make you uncomfortable, the couple can ask a family member or friend to do the reading. It's a win-win situation. This lets the officiant abstain from parts of the ceremony that make him or her uncomfortable, while giving the family or friends an important role.

reading during the ceremony

Although it's fine to have one or two people come up to do readings during the ceremony, it's important that they are in place and ready to go "live" when their time comes. Make sure that readers are in place in advance. You don't want the guests to have to wait while the readers make their way to-and-from the front of the room, and long moments of silence disrupt the flow of the ceremony.

selecting a prayer, blessing, or reading

We have included some examples of religious and spiritual readings that range from subtle and short, to longer options with more overtly religious overtones. The couple will know best what passages are a good fit, and if the passages provided here aren't suitable for the ceremony you are planning, visit the AMM website for more inspiration.

examples

Short and Interfaith

This special day is blessed _____ and _____, we
                                 Partner 1   Partner 2
pray that all your days together are blessed ones.

★ ★ ★

"God Shout-Out"

_____ and _____ come before God,
       Partner 1   *Partner 2*
their families, and their friends pledging their love and their hearts to one another.

The couple that first chose this option called it a, "God shout-out, rather than a God focus." If you choose this option, we recommend that you read it at the beginning of the *Words on Marriage* section (page 41). And, if you decide to also use the Short and Interfaith option above it, these two short blessings work well by reading the first one at the beginning of the Words on Marriage section, and the God Shout-Out at the end.

✦ ✦ ✦

Corinthians 13:4-8

Love is patient, love is kind. It does not envy, it does not boast, it is not proud. It is not rude, it is not self-seeking, it is not easily angered, it keeps no record of wrongs. Love does not delight in evil but rejoices with the truth. It always protects, always trusts, always hopes, always perseveres. Love never ends.

✦ ✦ ✦

Corinthians 13:4-8 - Couple Reading Variation

Partner 1: Love is patient.
Partner 2: Love is kind.
Partner 1: It does not envy. It does not boast.
Partner 2: It is not proud.
Partner 1: It is not rude, it is not self-seeking.
Partner 2: It is not easily angered, it keeps no record of wrongs.
Partner 1: Love does not delight in evil but rejoices with the truth.
Partner 2: It always protects, always trusts, always hopes, always perseveres.
Partner 1 & 2 Together: Love never ends.

✦ ✦ ✦

Ceremony Creation religious & spiritual words

Untitled, Spiritual Marriage Poem by unknown author
Bless our marriage, oh God,
as we begin our journey down the road of life together.
We don't know what lies ahead
for the road turns and bends.
But help us to make the best of whatever comes our way.
Help us to hug each other often…
laugh a lot, talk more, and argue less.
Help us to continue to enjoy each other
as we did when we first met.
Help us to realize that nothing nor no one is perfect
and to look for the good in all things,
And in all people, including ourselves.
Help us to respect each other's likes and dislikes,
opinions and beliefs, hopes and dreams and fears
even though we may not always understand them.
Help us to learn from each other and to help each other
to grow mentally, emotionally, and spiritually.
Help us to realize that there is design
and purpose in our lives as in the world
and no matter what happens to us
we will hold on to each other and know
that things have a way of working out for the good.
Help us to create for our children a peaceful, stable home
of love as a foundation on which they can build their lives.
But most of all, dear God, help us to keep lit
the torch of love that we now share in our hearts
so that by our loving example
we may pass on the light of love to our children
and to their children and to their
children's children forever.
Amen.

★★★

Why Marriage? by Mari Nichols-Haining

Because to the depths of me, I long to love one person,
With all my heart, my soul, my mind, my body...
Because I need a forever friend to trust with the intimacies of me,
Who won't hold them against me,
Who loves me when I'm unlikable,
Who sees the small child in me, and
Who looks for the divine potential of me...
Because I need to cuddle in the warmth of the night
With someone who thanks God for me,
With someone I feel blessed to hold...
Because marriage means opportunity
To grow in love and in friendship...
Because marriage is a discipline
To be added to a list of achievements...
Because marriages do not fail, people fail
When they enter into marriage
Expecting another to make them whole...
Because, knowing this,
I promise myself to take full responsibility
For my spiritual, mental and physical wholeness.
I create me,
I take half of the responsibility for my marriage
Together we create our marriage...
Because with this understanding
The possibilities are limitless.

★ ★ ★

Both of the following Irish Wedding Blessing options work well near the end of the ceremony, rather than early on. Consider using either blessing following the *Closing Remarks* (page 101), right before the Pronouncement.

Traditional Irish Wedding Blessing
May God go with you and bless you.
May you see your children's children.
May you be poor in misfortune.
May you be rich in blessings.
May you be slow to make enemies.
May you be quick to make friends.
But rich or poor, quick or slow
May you know nothing but happiness from this day forward.

Alternate Irish Wedding Blessing
May your mornings bring joy and your evenings bring peace.
May your troubles grow few as your blessings increase.
May the saddest day of your future
Be no worse than the happiest day of your past.
May your hands be forever clasped in friendship
And your hearts joined forever in love.
Your lives are very special,
God has touched you in many ways.
May his blessings rest upon you
And fill all your coming days.

5.5 Ceremony Creation
family & guest's blessings and remembrance

Many couples choose this moment to acknowledge close family, and others that have been there to watch them grow. This is the time in the ceremony to say a few words beyond, "thanks for being here." Most families appreciate this honor and acknowledgement, and this provides couples who are close to their families with a chance to recognize that closeness.

This can also be a time for remembrance, if a family member has recently passed.

> **in practice...**
> *Like many couples, Sam and Brenda wanted to use their ceremony as a chance to to honor their parents, and thank them for raising them to be the people that they had become.*
>
> *Brenda's grandmother had also passed away in the last year, and she wanted her memory to be a part of the wedding. And while the couple wanted to recognize Brenda's departed grandmother, it needed to be done in a way that didn't cast a somber mood over the ceremony – it was still a joyous occasion.*
>
> *Ultimately, Brenda chose to include a written acknowledgement in the ceremony program.*

expanding on the parent's blessing

Including an acknowledgment or blessing in the ceremony expands on the traditional bride's father's blessing, adding a modern dynamic that is increasingly popular these days. Most couples prefer this option since it establishes equality in their relationship by asking both partners' parents for their support, encouragement, and blessings, rather than just one partner's.

If the officiant or the couple are worried that they are wading into a quagmire of family politics, they can instead ask that their wedding be blessed by all the guests or eliminate this part of the ceremony altogether.

family & guests in attendance

For couples that want to ask family members or their guests for this blessing, there are a number of ways to include this in the ceremony. If done correctly, it's a participatory activity that adds a sense of collective purpose to the experience.

remembering the departed and distant

The family blessing is also an opportunity for the couple to recognize family members who are not at the ceremony. This may include relatives that have passed away or others that could not make it for any number of reasons.

If you choose to include a remembrance, we recommend that you do so in an upbeat way that celebrates that person's life (see sample included in the options below). Every piece contributes to the overall tone, and you don't want sadness to overwhelm the ceremony.

There are also ways to honor the departed outside of the ceremony. Some couples choose to place framed pictures of departed relatives on the welcome table in the reception area, or make a brief mention in the program.

examples

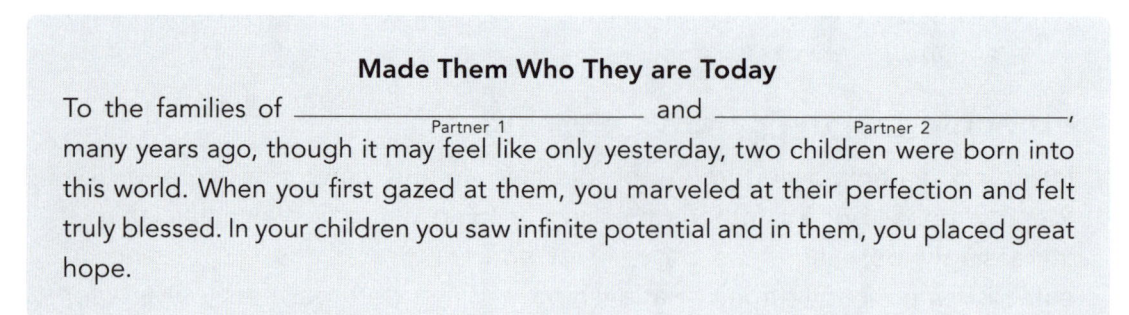

> **Made Them Who They are Today**
>
> To the families of _____ (Partner 1) and _____ (Partner 2), many years ago, though it may feel like only yesterday, two children were born into this world. When you first gazed at them, you marveled at their perfection and felt truly blessed. In your children you saw infinite potential and in them, you placed great hope.

With you they uttered their first words. With you they took their first steps. You rejoiced in their victories and cried with them in their grief. You guided them, nurtured them, educated them and loved them. You gave them all you had to give, so they would grow up strong and independent, capable of great love, which they share here today. Without you, this marriage [or union] would not, could not, be possible.

Today, all the love and caring you gave to _____ and
_{Partner 1}
_____, they will give to each other. And it does not end here.
_{Partner 2}
They will pass it along to the next generation. Families of the couple, we thank and honor you.

★★★

Merging of Families

Minister: This wedding is also a celebration of family. It is the merging of two families, separate up to this moment, but united from this day forward – uniting their different traditions and strengthening the family tree. To honor this uniting of the families, _____ and _____, wish to ask for their
_{Partner 1} _{Partner 2}
parents' blessing.

[To Partner 1's Parents]
_____, do you offer this couple your goodwill and support?
_{Parents' Names}
Partner 1's Parents: We do.

Minister: Do you welcome _____ as a member of your family
_{Partner 2}
and give him your love and affection?
Partner 1's Parents: We do.

[To Partner 2's Parents]
Minister: _____, do you offer this couple your goodwill
_{Parents' Names}
and support?
Partner 2's Parents: We do.

Minister: Do you welcome _____ as a member of your family
_{Partner 2}
and give her your love and affection?

Partner 2's Parents: We do.

✦ ✦ ✦

Alternate Merging of Families

Minister: We know that marriage is more than the joining of two people, it is the joining of two families, and therefore a celebration of that.

We now ask – who welcomes _____ as their daughter/
_{Partner 1}
child, and as a loving friend to _____?
_{Partner 2}

Partner 2's Family: We do.

Minister: Who welcomes _____ as a son, and as a loving
_{Partner 2}
friend to _____?
_{Partner 1}

Partner 1's Family: We do.

✦ ✦ ✦

Family and Friends Blessing

Minister: _____ and _____, you
_{Names of Partner 1's Parents}   _{Names of Partner 2's Parents}
recognize the significance of te commitment that _____ and
_{Partner 1}
_____ are about to make. They will be creating their own
_{Partner 2}
family and drawing on the lessons you shared with them throughout their lives. They will always be your children, but today the nature of that relationship will change. Your daughter is becoming a wife, and your son is becoming a husband.

Optional
Minister: Therefore, will you promise to give both of them your love, support, encouragement and heartfelt blessing? If so, please answer by saying "We will."

Parents: We will.

Minister: All of you, the family and friends of _____ (Partner 1) and _____ (Partner 2), recognize the significance of the commitment they are about to make. They will be creating their own family and drawing on the lessons that you have shared with them. Today, the nature of their relationships with you will change. Therefore, will you give both of them your love, support, encouragement, and heartfelt blessings? If so, please answer by saying "We will."

All Guests: We will.

✦ ✦ ✦

The honoring of the mothers with flowers can go after any of the above family blessings, if the couple wants an additional expression for their mothers, or it can be done as a stand-alone.

Honoring of the Mothers with Flowers

_____ (Partner 1) and _____ (Partner 2) will now present their mothers with flowers as symbols of their eternal gratitude.

[The couple jointly give a rose to each mother]

Thank you for your unconditional motherly love, for your unyielding strength in times of hardship, for the selfless sacrifices you have made for your children, and for always supporting them and providing wisdom and counsel as they grew from children into adults and became the people that they are today.

✦ ✦ ✦

If you are including a remembrance, such as the following examples, we have found that it works best immediately before one of the family blessings.

Remembrance: With Us in Spirit

_____ and _____ are grateful for the
        Partner 1   Partner 2
loved ones whose guidance and inspiration made them the people they are today. While some of those loved ones cannot be here with us today, _____
                                                                                                                           Partner 1
and _____ know that they are with us all in spirit, particularly
                     Partner 2
at this important time in their lives, as they build on the lessons of the living, and the departed, to create their own family.

⭐⭐⭐

Remembrance: Thankful for Their Contributions

At this time, _____ and _____ wish to
                                     Partner 1   Partner 2
thank all of you for joining them here today as they express their love for each other. They wish to honor each of you who has played a role in making them who they are today, and who they will grow to be as a family. We also wish to take this time to remember _____ with this beautiful verse.
                       Name or Names of Those Being Honored

Although death has separated us physically, faith and love have bound us eternally. Though we cannot see you, we know you are here. Though we cannot touch you, we feel the warmth of your smile, as we begin a new chapter in our lives. Today we pause to reflect upon those who have shaped our character, molded our spirits and touched our hearts. May this verse be a reminder of the memories we have shared, a representation of the everlasting impact you have made upon our lives.

5.6 Ceremony Creation
words on marriage

The words on marriage section of the ceremony is similar to the opening remarks section, but tends to be more general in its words, tone, and meaning. This may include the officiant's own observations, a compelling quote about marriage, or a reading from the *Readings* chapter (page 83) of this book.

> **in practice...**
> *When Golda and Azar were discussing their ceremony, they agreed that the lifelong commitment that they were entering into should be front-and-center. They knew that they wanted words on marriage read aloud that communicated how they felt about the bond they were entering into.*

This section of the ceremony is usually about a paragraph in length, and is focused on the meaning of marriage and the importance of commitment.

examples

Shared Joys and Sorrows

_____ (Partner 1) and _____ (Partner 2) come before us pledging their love and their hearts to one another. May they be true and loving; may their hearts be filled with kindness and understanding, may they forgive each other's weaknesses, and laugh together often. May they be friends, companions, and partners, continuing to meet the joys and sorrows of life as one. As the years pass, and they move from one chapter in their life together to the next, may their love continue to deepen and mature, and may their home forever be a place of love and joy.

★★★

Love and Support

Marriage is not something entered into lightly since it requires that each person be willing to support the other in both good times, and in bad. Marriage requires that each person, at times, put their wishes and needs second to those of their partner. One partner may need to laugh at jokes that aren't funny or eat food that is not to their taste. But in return, marriage provides a level of joy that one person by themselves cannot reach and, a type of love that only two people can create together.

★ ★ ★

Lighthearted

In today's world, there are plenty of wonderful ways for a couple to spend their lives together that don't include marriage. So why get married? Is it an excuse to throw a great party? A way to get friends and family from far away to visit? Those things certainly matter, but it's deeper than that. From where I stand, marriage is one partner promising to the other that in addition to loving them, they want to commit themselves to the other for the rest of their lives. It is stating that they will be there for their partner when they need them most. That they will provide comfort, a kind word, and a shoulder to cry on. And when times are good, as we hope they always are, it's a promise that the two of them will be there to laugh together. Marriage is saying that not only do you want to be partners, you want to be partners for life.

★ ★ ★

Spiritual Bond

_____ and _____ are getting married
Partner 1 Partner 2
today. Although marriage is in some ways just another step in their relationship, it is the most important one they will ever take. In getting married, they are agreeing to a bond that is not only legal, but spiritual. It is a bond that unites their hearts and minds into a lifelong partnership that is stronger than two individuals alone can ever be. It is a public act, that we are all witnesses to. But marriage is so much more than speaking promises and signing a document. Marriage is an eternal vow, and no matter what the world might say, these two people have pledged themselves to each other. A pledge to face whatever comes their way, together. A pledge to support each other, nurture each other, and love each other for the rest of their lives.

★★★

The Rollercoaster of Love

Being married is like riding a roller coaster. Today, after a short or long wait in line, these two individuals are strapping themselves in for the ride. It may have started with a thrill, but chances are it starts with a slow climb and building anticipation. The roller coaster of marriage will have its ups and its downs. One minute you are flying, excitement and thrills abound, and the next, you are creeping back up or coasting along, enjoying a break from the chaos. But what makes marriage wonderful is that you are not riding alone, you have a partner alongside you who is there holding your hand, whispering calming words, or screaming in excitement. And, like a good roller coaster, you never want to get off.

★★★

Poetic

A lifetime bond. A commitment to each other for eternity. A lifelong embrace. All are wonderful, and applicable, ways to describe marriage. But marriage is also about the little things. The warm smile your partner gives you when you most need it most. The hug that calms your nerves. The laughter that lightens the moment. And of course, the kiss that lets you know that you are in this together. Marriage is committing to not only a lifetime together, but to be there for the other person at any moment. To provide the support that your partner needs. Marriage is a bond created on a single day that is renewed every day thereafter, through thought and action.

quotes on love and commitment

A great spouse loves you exactly as you are. An extraordinary spouse helps you grow; inspires you to be, do and give your very best.
— Fawn Weaver

✦✦✦

We come to love not by finding a perfect person, but by learning to see an imperfect person perfectly.
— Sam Keen

✦✦✦

Love doesn't make the world go round. Love is what makes the ride worthwhile.
— Unknown

✦✦✦

Love is the greatest gift when given. It is the highest honor when received.
— Fawn Weaver

✦✦✦

Coming together is a beginning; keeping together is progress; working together is success.
— Henry Ford

✦✦✦

A great marriage is not when the 'perfect couple' comes together. It is when an imperfect couple learns to enjoy their differences.
— Dave Meurer

✦✦✦

Marriage is a commitment— a decision to do, all through life, that which will express your love for one's spouse.
— Herman H. Kieval

★ ★ ★

Happily ever after is not a fairy tale. It's a choice.
— Fawn Weaver

★ ★ ★

Love is a partnership of two unique people who bring out the very best in each other, and who know that even though they are wonderful as individuals, they are even better together.
— Barbara Cage

★ ★ ★

You meet thousands of people and none of them really touch you, and then you meet one person and your life is changed forever.
— Jamie Randall, from the movie, Love and Other Drugs

★ ★ ★

You don't marry one person; you marry three: the person you think they are, the person they are, and the person they are going to become as a result of being married to you.
— Richard Needham

★ ★ ★

A happy marriage doesn't mean you have a perfect spouse or a perfect marriage. It

simply means you've chosen to look beyond the imperfections in both.
— Fawn Weaver

★ ★ ★

Chains do not hold a marriage together. It is threads, hundreds of tiny threads which sew people together through the years.
— Simone Signoret

★ ★ ★

Marriage is not a noun; it's a verb. It isn't something you get. It's something you do. It's the way you love your partner every day.
— Barbara De Angelis

★ ★ ★

Love doesn't sit there like a stone, it has to be made, like bread; remade every day, made new.
— Ursula LeGuin

★ ★ ★

The more things we can laugh about, the more alive we become: The more things we can laugh about together, the more connected we become.
— Frank Pittman

★ ★ ★

I love being married. It's so great to find that one special person you want to annoy for the rest of your life.
— Rita Rudner

★★★

Love is the condition in which the happiness of another person is essential to your own.
— Robert Heinlein

★★★

Love is like a friendship caught on fire. In the beginning a flame, very pretty, often hot and fierce, but still only light and flickering. As love grows older, our hearts mature, and our love becomes as coals, deep burning and unquenchable.
— Joseph Addison

★★★

One of the most amazing gifts in life is to find someone who knows all your flaws, differences, and mistakes, yet still loves everything about you.
— Unknown

★★★

Nothing feels better than when you love someone with your whole heart and soul and they love you back even more.
— Karen Kostyla

★★★

Rules for a happy marriage:
1. Never both be angry at the same time.
2. Never yell at each other unless the house is on fire.
3. If one of you has to win an argument, let it be your spouse.
4. If you have to criticize, do it lovingly.

5. Never bring up mistakes from the past.
6. Neglect the whole world rather than each other.
7. Never go to sleep with an argument unsettled.
8. At least once a day say a kind word or pay a compliment to your partner.
9. When you have done something wrong, admit it and ask for forgiveness.
10. It takes two to make a quarrel, and the one in the wrong is usually the one who does the most talking.
— Unknown

★★★

The goal in marriage is not to think alike, but to think together.
— Robert C. Dodds

★★★

Love is just a word until someone comes along and gives it meaning.
— Unknown

★★★

Lean on each other's strengths. Forgive each other's weaknesses.
— Unknown

★★★

Good relationships don't just happen. They take time, patience, and two people who truly want to be together.
— Unknown

★★★

Being someone's first love may be great, but to be their last is beyond perfect.
— Unknown

★ ★ ★

Happy marriages begin when we marry the ones we love, and they blossom when we love the ones we marry.
— Tom Mullen

★ ★ ★

It's always nice to have someone in your life who can make you smile even when they're not around.
— Unknown

★ ★ ★

Marriage does not guarantee you will be together forever, it's only paper. It takes love, respect, trust, understanding, friendship and faith in your relationship to make it last.
— Unknown

5.7 Ceremony Creation
the couple's story

The couple's story is one of the most important parts of the ceremony – it is a glimpse into their shared history, a window into their relationship. During this part of the ceremony, the officiant tells the couple's story, but in their words. Guests are naturally curious, and a compelling narrative helps them understand why they are celebrating.

> **in practice...**
> *For Kelly and Shannon, the way in which they met and began dating was a defining feature of their relationship, and something that they wanted to communicate to their guests. It was a large wedding, with its share of casual acquaintances, and this was a chance to draw everyone in.*
>
> *[See their full example at the end of this section.]*

People want a personal ceremony, one that's tailored to their relationship, and not something generic delivered by an officiant going through the motions of an insert-name-here ceremony.

preserving the couple's voice

Not everyone will be as forthcoming as Kelly and Shannon were, and recording and compiling these stories is sometimes the toughest and most time-consuming part of your officiating duties. Nonetheless, we encourage you to give some serious thought to the couple's story and who they are together. A little extra effort now, and people will be talking about this wedding for decades, we promise!

When the time comes for you to recount these stories to the assembled guests, it's important that you preserve the voices of the couple. Since you are incorporating anecdotes spoken in the couple's own words, you will probably need to edit their responses for grammar and clarity, but you still want the guests to know that it is them speaking. For example, you can say, "Shannon remembers their first date, and the way that Kelly wouldn't stop talking about politics…"

This doesn't mean your narrative should have the audience cringing with embarrassment either. To the contrary, such stories should only be recounted if the couple insists (and usually they don't!). Leave the bawdy tales for the best man and maid of honor speeches later, when the champagne is flowing. Others can get away with that sort of behavior. As an officiant, there are certain standards of conduct that should be upheld.

work with the couple to prepare

Your first step should be to provide the couple with questions about themselves and their relationship. Below are some questions to get the couple thinking, but these can be tailored on a case-by-case basis. For the best results, have each partner answer separately. Having two distinct voices makes the story more impactful. It's as simple as emailing the questions to each partner and asking them to email them back to you, separately. You can also hand them the questions during the *Planning With the Couple* (page 13).

For best results, if the couple answer their questions separately, don't share this part of the ceremony during the draft review process. This way, their answers are a surprise to each other, and heard for the first time during ceremony. It makes for a touching and humorous moment.

questions for the couple

- What attracted you to your partner?
- How did you get engaged?
- How would you describe your relationship?
- How do you describe your partner to people who are hearing about them for the first time?
- What makes you smile when you think about your partner?

- What are you most looking forward to about your life together (after the wedding) and what do you see when you think about your longer-term future together?

If the couple have a great "how they met" story or an interesting first date story, you can ask about those as well. Otherwise, these questions are sure to elicit some great memories and thoughts that you can include in the ceremony.

putting it all together

The optimal length of this section is between three and five minutes, so it's likely going to take some heavy editing to condense the couple's answers to fit. You don't want this part to take up too much time, but you also don't want to remove anecdotes and observations that provide meaningful insight into the couple's lives.

Your goal should be to provide guests with insight into who the couple are together. The point is never to embarrass the couple. Many in attendance will only know one partner, and they'll be interested to see who their friend, colleague, or old classmate is marrying. This is your chance to make that connection.

As you're going over their replies, consider using the "Grandparents' Filter." What will the grandparents want to hear? They'll appreciate words like "beautiful" and "attractive," but you might cause offense with words like, "hot" and "sexy."

Anecdotes such as these would normally be met with an eye-roll, but these sorts of stories resonate at at wedding, especially when told by a third party. Families appreciate knowing that their loved ones are adored, cared for, and respected by their future spouse, and these stories are a great way to communicate that.

So, while this exercise takes some preparation, couples often enjoy the experience. Revisiting the way that they met, and the best attributes of their future spouse, tends to remind couples of why they decided to get married in the first place.

shannon & kelly's story
The Introduction

Before the couple exchange their vows, I want to take a few minutes to share some memories that the couple shared with me, that allow us to understand the journey that brought them to this moment today. What brought them together, what are they really like as a couple, and what sort of future are they looking forward to together?

There's always "two sides to every story", but that's part of what makes this fun! And the best part is, they will be hearing each other's answers for the first time.

1 - How The Couple Met

What attracted them to each other?

For **Shannon** it was, "**Kelly's** beauty, her smile, and how easily we connected."

For **Kelly** it was, "how comfortable I felt with him from the start, and how smart, funny, and interesting he was to be around."

2 - Their Relationship

How do they describe their relationship?

Kelly says that their relationship is, "easy-going." Here's how she put it: "We communicate well and remain honest with each other, handling anything that comes up right away. Everything has felt easy together, and we were always completely comfortable with each other and ourselves. I didn't have to sacrifice myself, or my career, personality or space to keep him happy. I can be me, he can him, and we can just be us – no expectations, just happiness."

Shannon says that, "I would say we are fun light-hearted, and very loving. Always helping each other no matter what the issue is. There for each other for anything. True Love."

3 - Their Love for Each Other

How do they describe the other, and what makes them smile when they think about them?

For **Kelly** "I tell people he is profoundly in touch with the world around him, very sweet natured and loves to cook. I just smile thinking about his kind face with a genuine smile."

For **Shannon** "I describe her as the love of my life. I had been looking for her for many years, then stumbled upon her. I mention that 'you' will love her; she is sweet and has a kind heart. She is also fun and spunky and will kick your butt if she has to."

4 - The Proposal

So, how did they get engaged?

Shannon recalls, "I took her to visit the old country and I sprung the question while we were staying in a 12th century home that belonged to my cousin…"

Kelly adds, "I can't believe his relatives knew what was going to happen. I had no clue."

5 - Plans for the Future

What are they most looking forward to about their life together, and what do they see when they think about their longer-term future together?

For **Shannon** "A fun honeymoon adventure that leads into all of the normal life things that we have dreamed about."

For **Kelly** "Two kids, one dog, and Shannon by my side."

The Conclusion

It's clear that these two were made for each other and that they have an exciting future ahead of them. I know I speak for everyone here when I say that their future together is a future that we are all excited about, and look forward to being a part of!

5.8 Ceremony Creation
VOWS

The exchange of vows is the reason for the wedding day, and the promises made are supposed to last a lifetime.

Vows need only answer the basic question, "How do I feel about my life partner, and what promises do I want to make for our life together?" It can be as serious or as funny as the couple wants - it's often a combination of both - what matters is that the choice reflects the couple and their relationship.

vow format options

While most couples will personalize their vows in one way or another, the exchange generally takes one of the following forms:

1. **Reading to Each Other** - The vows are read by the couple, to each other. The couples can read their vows from cards, or memorize them (see *Directing the Ceremony* section, page 125). For couples that choose to read from note cards, the officiant can hand them their lines when the time comes.
2. **Repeat After Me** - The vows are first read by the officiant, and the couple then repeats them in phrases.
3. **Question(s)** - The vows are a question or multiple questions, which the officiant reads, and the couple answers with either "I do," or "I will" or a combination of both.

Most ceremonies feature the first option, since it allows couples to express their feelings and make authentic promises to each other. The third option is popular with couples that don't enjoy speaking in front of large groups, only requiring them to say, "I do," while the officiant does the heavy lifting.

> **in practice...**
> *Neither Aisha nor her fiance Murat were especially excited about the idea of public speaking, but to both of them, limiting their vows to "I do" oversimplified*

their complex feelings for each other. In addition to detailing their love for each other, the couple wanted to inject humor and feeling into the vows.

Murat was concerned about bungling his lines, and Aisha was worried about the optics of squinting at her lines in front of their guests. As a compromise, they chose to repeat their vows after the officiant and then close out that part of the ceremony by answering with the iconic "I do" vows. Their solution allowed them to use more detailed vows, without the possibility of misreading or forgetting lines.

structuring the vow exchange

Ultimately, there's a lot of flexibility here. Couples can choose any of the three options or combine them to suit their needs. For the couple that always imagined themselves saying, "I do," but who also want to include personal vows, they can start out by reading vows to each other and then transition to answering "I do" questions. Another option is to start out by answering the "I do" questions, and then exchanging "repeat after me" vows.

The couple can both use the same vows, which they recite to each other, or they can each read different vows that highlight their feelings towards their partner.

Many of these examples are borrowed from specific weddings that involved the union of a bride and a groom. While Aishe and Murat's wedding was more traditional, feel free to swap out their names, or the designations "bride," and "groom" with "partner" or "spouse," or any other words that you choose.

selecting vows

This book features a wide range of vows for couples, because we know that drafting your own from scratch can be intimidating. And even if you have some ideas, our examples might help you put those thoughts into words.

Couples that choose to write their own vows usually do so because they want their words to reflect the nuances of their relationship. The examples we provide have been sourced from hundreds of weddings, featuring straight and LGBTQ couples, and use language that reflects the original ceremony. You should think of designations such as "husband," "wife," or "partner" as placeholders. If a set of vows appeals to the couple, then by all means, use them!

If the couple choose to use the "I do" option for their vows, we recommend three to six questions, with a mixture of serious/touching ones and funny/personal ones. It doesn't matter who speaks their vows first, but it helps if the partner most prone to tearing up – or crying – goes first.

As mentioned in the *Get Ordained!* chapter (page 3), it is generally a requirement that ceremonies include a declaration of intent, or "I do." That said, you can still write personal vows and use them in combination with the required declaration of intent.

examples
timeless vows

Classic

I, _____ (Partner 1) take you, _____ (Partner 2) to be my (husband/wife/partner), to have and to hold, for better and for worse, for richer and for poorer, in sickness and in health, to love and to cherish, from this day forward, until death do us part.

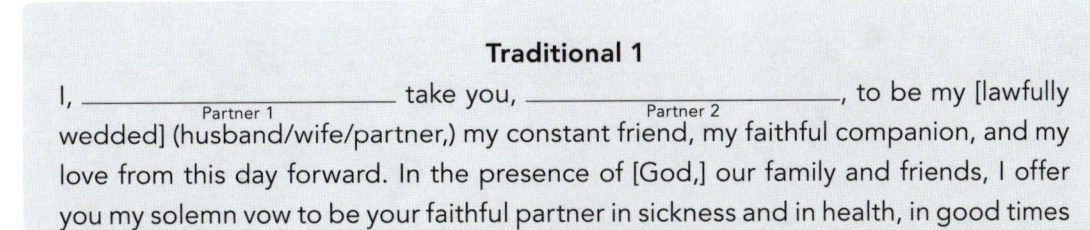

★ ★ ★

Traditional 1

I, _____ (Partner 1) take you, _____ (Partner 2), to be my [lawfully wedded] (husband/wife/partner,) my constant friend, my faithful companion, and my love from this day forward. In the presence of [God,] our family and friends, I offer you my solemn vow to be your faithful partner in sickness and in health, in good times and in bad, and in joy as well as in sorrow. I promise to love you unconditionally, to support you in your goals, to honor and respect you, to laugh with you and cry with you, and to cherish you for as long as we both shall live.

★★★

Traditional 2

_____, I take you to be my lawfully wedded (husband/wife/
          Name of Partner
partner). Before these witnesses, I vow to love you and care for you as long as we both shall live. I take you with all your faults and your strengths as I offer myself to you with all my faults and strengths. I will help you when you need help, and I will turn to you when I need help. I choose you as the person with whom I will spend my life.

★★★

Traditional 3

I, _____ take you, _____, to be my beloved
         Partner 1   Partner 2
(husband/wife/partner), to have and to hold you, to honor you, to treasure you, to be at your side in sorrow and in joy, in the good times, and in the bad, and to love and cherish you always. I promise you this from my heart, for all the days of my life.

★★★

A Modern Take on Tradition

I, _____ take you, _____, to be my (husband/
          Partner   Partner 2
wife/partner), to respect, cherish and honor, to laugh with you in joy, to grieve with you in sorrow, to grow with you in love, and from this day forward, I will share my life with you.

contemporary vows

Best Friend

I love you. You are my best friend. Today I give myself to you in marriage. I promise to encourage and inspire you, to laugh with you, and to comfort you in times of sorrow and struggle. I promise to love you in good times and in bad, when life seems easy and when it seems hard, when our love is simple, and when it is an effort. I promise to cherish you, and to always hold you in highest regard. This I promise to you today, and for all the days of our life together.

★ ★ ★

Love & Cherish

I, _____ (Partner 1) take you, _____ (Partner 2), to be my (husband/wife), my partner in life and my one true love. I will cherish our friendship and love you today, tomorrow, and forever. I will trust you and honor you I will laugh with you and cry with you. I will love you faithfully; through the best and the worst, through the difficult and the easy. No matter what may come, I will always be there for you. As I have given you my hand to hold, so I give you my life to keep.

★ ★ ★

Proclamation of Love

I, _____ (Partner 1) take you, _____ (Partner 2), to be my (wife/husband/partner), knowing in my heart that you will be my constant friend, my faithful partner in life, and my one true love. On this special day, I give to you in the presence of [God and] our families and friends my sacred promise to stay by your side as your (wife/husband/partner), in sickness and in health, in joy and in sorrow, as well as through the good times and the bad. I promise to love you without reservation, honor and respect you, provide for your needs to the best of my abilities, protect you from harm, comfort you in times of distress, grow with you in mind and spirit, always be open and honest with you, and cherish you for as long as we both shall live.

★ ★ ★

Short & Sweet

I, _____ take you, _____, to be my (wife/
        Partner 1   Partner 2
husband/partner), knowing in my heart that you will be my constant friend, my faithful partner, and one true love. You are my best friend and I will love and respect you always.

★★★

Cherish

I love you. You are my best friend. Today I give myself to you in marriage. I promise to encourage and inspire you, to laugh with you, and to comfort you in times of sorrow and struggle. I promise to love you in good times and in bad, when life seems easy and when it seems hard, when our love is simple, and when it requires effort. I promise to cherish you, and to always hold you in highest regard. These things I give to you today, and all the days of our life.

★★★

Support

From this day forward, I promise you these things. I will laugh with you in times of joy and comfort you in times of sorrow. I will share in your dreams, and support you as you strive to achieve your goals. I will listen to you with compassion and understanding, and speak to you with encouragement. I will help you when you need it, and step aside when you don't. I will remain faithful to you for better or worse, in times of sickness and health. You are my best friend and I will love and respect you always.

★★★

True Love Found

I have finally discovered the meaning of real love. For as long as I live I will love, respect, and honor you. I will be committed to self-growth and to the growth of our relationship. I promise to be honest and to communicate my needs and feelings, just as I promise to listen to yours. I will be faithful to you in mind, body, and spirit. I will be your friend and life partner no matter what life brings to us. Today, I pledge my commitment to you.

★★★

From this Day Forward
Today I will marry my best friend, the one I will live with, dream with, and love. I take you to be my (husband/wife/partner). From this day forward I will cherish you, I will look with joy down the path that leads to tomorrow, knowing we will walk it together, side by side, hand in hand, and heart to heart.

★★★

Love Everything About You
I promise to give you the best of myself and to ask of you no more than you can give. I promise to accept you the way you are. I fell in love with you for the qualities, abilities, and outlook on life that you have, and I won't try to reshape you in a different image. I promise to respect you as a person with your own interests, desires, and needs, and to realize that those are sometimes different, but no less important than my own. I promise to keep myself open to you, to let you see through the window of my personal world into my innermost fears and feelings, secrets and dreams. I promise to grow along with you, to be willing to face change as we both change in order to keep our relationship alive and exciting. And finally, I promise to love you in good times and in bad, with all I have to give and all I feel inside in the only way I know how... completely and forever.

★★★

You're My Inspiration
_____, you have filled my world with meaning. You have
 Partner's Name
made me happier and more fulfilled. Thank you for taking me as I am, loving me,

and welcoming me into your heart. I promise to always love you, respect you as an individual, and to be faithful to you forever. Today I choose you to be my partner, and commit myself to you for the rest of my life.

★★★

Found the Perfect Partner

Today, I want you to know how lucky I feel for having found the one perfect person for me, the one who suits me so perfectly, who gives me boundless hope, and fills me with anticipation for the future. Every day we're together, you do nothing but make me happy. The day we met was the day I became truly alive again, and on this day — our wedding day — I declare my love and devotion for you before the entire world. I make a vow to stand by your side through the best and worst of times, and to give you the best of what I have from now until the end of our days.

★★★

serious, funny, personal, & everything in between

#1 Fan

_____ (Partner's Name), I take you as my (husband/wife/partner), my best friend in life and my one true love. I promise to be your lover and best friend today, tomorrow, and forever. I will love you faithfully through laughter and tears, through joy and sorrow, and I will stand by your side even if (favorite team) are playing. I will trust you and I will honor you, I will laugh with you and I will cry with you, especially when the (favorite team) lose. Come what may, I will always be there for you. As I have given you my hand to hold, so I give you my life to keep. You are my soulmate and I promise to love you with everything I am from this day forward and for eternity.

★★★

Happy Home

_____ (Partner's Name), it seems like an eternity since I first moved my furniture into your living room, but it also feels like it was only yesterday, at the same time. I'm blessed to be spending the rest of my life with someone as loving, caring, generous, and giving as you. I'm looking forward to round bellies, Saturday soccer, and all the other joys of family life. You add a dimension to my existence that I never knew existed, and I'm lucky to be sharing my life with you. _____ — \[Partner's Name\] with all my love, I take you to be my (wife/husband/partner). I promise to love you, to remain committed to you, and to support you. I promise to be patient, a listener, and a communicator. I promise to hold you when you're sad and laugh with you when you're happy. I pledge to help make your dreams come true, because they are ours now. And finally, I promise to be your best friend and love you always.

★★★

Falling in Love Each Day

_____, long ago, when I first imagined this day, what it would \[Partner's Name\] feel like, and the person that would be standing beside me, I couldn't have imagined how perfect this moment would feel. You are everything and more than I could want in a partner for life. True love like this is rare and difficult to find, but I know that I have found it in you. In the time that's passed since our first meeting, my life has changed for the better because of you. You have introduced me to possibilities that I didn't know existed. You have pushed me and challenged me to do things that I didn't know I was capable of. You have a passion for life that inspires me to be the best person I can be. You are self-confident and know what you want in life, and I admire you for that. When I look at you my heart melts. When you smile, there's a sparkle in your eyes that I find both irresistible and comforting, and I find myself falling in love with you more and more each day. You are my best friend, my confidant, and my one true love. Thank you for loving me unconditionally. In turn, I promise to love and respect you, to support you and be by your side, no matter what challenges life sends our way. I look forward to spending the rest of my life with you and building a family together. Today my dreams have come true. I love you now, always and forever.

★★★

Perfect for Each Other

_____, I love you now and promise to love you for the rest of
       Partner's Name
my life. You are my best friend and will be forever. I appreciate you for who you are, and for how you have made me a better person. I promise to be true to you in good times and in bad. I promise to be patient, supportive, understanding, and always honest. I promise to be the one who always warms your hands and feet, who offers a comforting shoulder to lean on. I am so lucky to have found the perfect partner, someone who fits me, and who accepts me for who I am. I can't promise to be perfect, but I promise to be perfect for you and to be by your side forever.

★★★

It's About Time!

Today, one of my dreams is coming true. I am so honored to marry you… and it's about time! I will love you today, tomorrow, and forever. I am so lucky and grateful that you chose me to be part of my life. I promise to help you follow your dreams, and I will always believe in you. I promise to always hug you and kiss you, each and every day. I will be there for you with my whole heart, especially through the hard times. I will do my best to always listen, and you know how hard that is for me! I will never leave you, and will always be by your side. I hope to always make you laugh and have fun. The obstacles we endure will challenge both of us, but I know they will make us stronger. We are like food and wine. We may not pair perfectly, but we will always bring out the best in each other. We were meant to be with each other. Today, I promise to be fully committed and respectful of not only you, but our relationship. I cannot promise that I'll never steal your food, hog the sheets, or take over the bathroom cabinet, but I promise you today that I will always honor you and support you. I truly believe that fate lead me to you, and I cannot wait to build my life with you – my soulmate, my best friend, my (husband/wife/partner).

★★★

Looking Forward to Every Day

On our first date, I knew I was in trouble. You were the most interesting person I had ever met. Different, intriguing, and I needed to know more. As time went on, it became clear that we had something special. And here we are, on our wedding day, making it official. Throughout our relationship, that spark has remained. When I pull into the driveway, I feel giddy knowing that you're waiting inside to greet me. When I have a bad dream, I reach for you in the darkness, and I feel safe again. If I'm in a bad mood, I know that you'll make me laugh again. You're my lover, my protector and my best friend. This is why I'm marrying you, because I can't imagine spending a second of my life without you.

★★★

Comrades

_____ (Partner's Name), in the presence of our family and friends, I take you to be my (wife/husband/partner). I promise to be your partner, lover, companion, and friend; I'll be your greatest ally, your biggest fan, and your toughest critic. Your comrade in adventure and your accomplice in mischief. I vow to laugh with you in joy, to be your comfort in sorrow and to turn to you in my times of need. I promise to grow with you, and never lose sight of the little things. And, I promise to love, respect, and cherish you through all of our days.

★★★

Hot Tub Promise

_____ (Partner's Name), I take you as my (wife/husband/partner), my best friend, and the love of my life. I promise to love, honor, and respect you; to appreciate you for who you are and to support you in all your endeavors. I promise to create a home with you filled with creativity, compassion, and joy. I promise that home will have a hot tub, someday. I will be your faithful partner in sickness and in health. I will love you and stand with you in times of happiness as well as in sorrow. For as long as I live, I will be there for you. With you at my side, and I am looking forward to sharing the rest of our lives together.

★★★

The Nitty Gritty

My love _____, when I met you, one of the first things you
                 Partner's Name
taught me was how to take one step at a time. Through this lesson, I have been grown as a person, while developing our relationship as a couple. This allowed me to fall in love in a way I'd never imagined. I am excited to choose you as the person I will spend my life with. You make me laugh and your zest for life inspires me. You pay attention to the little details. It told me a lot about you when I found toilet paper facing the way I like it! Today, I promise to love you without reservation, in good times and in bad, when life is easy and when it's hard, when love is simple and when it takes some effort. I promise to respect you as an individual, and as we grow together as a couple. I promise to encourage you to achieve your goals and to help us in reaching the goals we set together. I love what I know and trust what I don't, and I am so excited to fall in love with you a little more every single day.

★★★

Your Biggest Cheerleader

_____, you are my heart, my love, and my best friend. I am
        Partner's Name
so lucky to have you in my life. My world is balanced because of you. I have always felt the freedom to be myself around you. I promise to be there for you when you are down, to make you laugh when you need cheering up, to support you and always be by your side. I will support your dreams as you have supported mine. I will respect you as you have respected me. I will always be there to comfort you. I will never take your love for granted and I'll always keep it real. No one is perfect, but you are perfect for me.

★★★

By Your Side

_____, as I look at you, standing here with me, I know I have
        Partner's Name
found my soulmate. Since the day we met, I knew that we shared a special kind of love, a love focused on our relationship, not on ourselves. I knew that I had found the perfect companion that I wanted to keep in my life forever. You have been there for

me when I needed you the most, and I promise to do the same for you. I promise to be faithful, that we will laugh more than we cry, and that I will always be the person you can count on. As our love grew, I knew you would be the (mother/father) of my children, and I am so excited for that chapter of our life to begin. I want to spend every waking moment by your side, and have you by mine. Let our goal be to follow in our grandparents' footsteps, sharing the length of our lives with each other, as they have done (or did, in the event they have passed away). I truly believe that nothing can get in our way of finding true happiness. The only thing I need in this life is to have you by my side, every step of the way, sharing life with you, laughing with you, and dancing with you. You are my favorite! I am so lucky to be able to call you my (wife/husband/partner). I love you!

★★★

The Long View

We stand here today, in the presence of our family and friends, to declare our commitment and make vows of unending love. These vows are more than just words – they are a recognition that you are a part of my soul, an extension of myself that I carry you with me always. You are my best friend; you are my partner in life and my true match. You pick me up when I fall; when I get ahead of myself, you remind me to slow down; when I am lost, you help me find my way again; when I am lazy, you challenge me; and when I am sad, you make me laugh, even if I don't want to. Patiently, lovingly, kindly, you accept me as I am. There is no other person who can do what you do for me; from the smallest everyday acts of kindness to grand gestures, you always find a way to show your devotion. I hope that during our years together as (partners/husband and wife/spouses), I am able to show you the same level of care and affection that you have shown me during our years together. To start with, I promise to do more dishes, help with the laundry, and perhaps even cook dinner more often. More importantly, I promise to stand by you, to listen to you, to support your dreams and goals, to share the joy of our successes and to bear the burden of our losses, to work beside you in growing our lives together, to respect you, and love you as my best friend, my beloved, and now my (husband/wife/partner for life). I make these vows today, not just as my word, but as a piece of my soul that you will carry with you always.

★★★

Anything's Possible

In the time since I met you, my life has changed for the better. You have introduced me to possibilities that I didn't know existed. You have challenged me to do things that I didn't think I could do. You have a passion for life that inspires me to be the best person I can be. When I look at you, my heart melts. Your smile brings out a sparkle in your eyes that is irresistible and comforting and I find myself falling in love with you more and more with each passing day. You are my best friend, my confidant and my one true love.

★★★

Crazy in Love

Because of you, I laugh, I smile, and I dream. I love how you are always up for whatever crazy plan I have. When I think about our future together, it brings a smile to my face. I look forward to spending the rest of my life with you, caring for you, nurturing you, going on adventures with you, being there for you and experiencing all that life has in store for us. You are my best friend, my confidant, and my one true love.

combination vows

You can arrange these vows in any order. For example, one partner can read his or her personal vows, followed by the second partner's personal vows. Once they have both read their vows, the officiant can ask the couple their "I do" vows. Alternatively, the officiant can begin with the "I do" questions, after which the couple can read their personal vows. In the two examples below, one partner reads their personal vows and then answers "I do," after which the process is then repeated for the other partner.

Laugh at Each Other's Jokes

Minister: Will you take _____ to be your husband; will you love,
                            Partner 2

honor, and cherish him, now and forevermore?

Partner 1: I will.

Minister: Do you promise to hold _____ [Partner 2's] hand, look him in the eyes, and listen to his hopes, dreams and thoughts?

Partner 1: I do.

Minister: Do you promise to always laugh at his goofy jokes?

Partner 1: I do.

Minister: Will you take _____ [Partner 1] to be your wife; will you love, honor, and cherish her, now and forevermore?

Partner 2: I will.

Minister: Do you promise to hold _____ [Partner 1's] hand, listen to her needs, and do the little things that brighten her day?

Partner 2: I do.

Minister: Do you promise to tease her, make silly jokes, and come up with new, creative ways to drive her crazy?

Partner 2: I do.

★★★

Lighthearted Daily Life Promises

Bride: _____ [Groom's Name], as we stand here today in the presence of our family and friends, I make these vows to you. You are my best friend, my partner, and my favorite. When I fall down, you pick me up. When I get ahead of myself, you remind me to slow down. When I cry, you remind me to smile. I promise to encourage and inspire you, hold your hand through all of life's circumstances, through the bitter and the sweet. I will share your dreams and support your goals. I vow to talk and to listen, to build a home with you filled with harmony, happiness, and love. I promise to get you Mexican food at nine o'clock at night. I promise not to sing too loudly in the car – as long as you promise to always drive on road trips. I look forward to becoming your co-pilot. If you wash the dog, I'll dry. If you wash the laundry, I'll fold.

And if you cook dinner, I'll wash the dishes. I promise to be a true and faithful friend to you now, always, and forever. These are my vows to you.

Minister: Do you, _____ (Bride's Name), take _____ (Groom's Name) to be your husband, to appreciate and cherish him, as long as you both shall live?
Bride: I do.

Groom: _____ (Bride's Name), standing here surrounded by our friends and family, I make these vows to you. Through every step that we have taken to get here, you have helped me become who I am today, and you continue to bring out the best in me. Thank you for putting up with my stubbornness and encouraging my dreams. You are the best part of me, the person I want to wake up beside every day, and my partner in life. I promise to move anywhere with you because I know that my home is with you. I promise to love and support you as you pursue your goals and aspirations, to hold you close when times are good and even closer when times are bad. I vow to help make a home together where our dreams can flourish. I promise to rub your feet after a long day, to make the coffee every morning, and to do all the driving on road trips if you will be the navigator. I promise to listen to your needs, to be a patient partner and a faithful husband, now and always. These are my vows to you.

Minister: Do you _____ (Groom's Name), take _____ (Bride's Name) to be your wife, to love and comfort her, for as long as you both shall live?
Groom: I do.

★★★

Here For You

Minister: _____ (Brides's Name), do you give yourself to _____ (Groom's Name) in marriage?
Bride: I do.

Minister: Do you promise to encourage him, inspire him, laugh with him, and comfort him in times of sorrow and struggle?
Bride: I do.

Minister: Do you promise to love him in good times and bad, when life seems easy and when it seems hard, when love is simple, and when it is complicated?
Bride: I do.

Minister: Do you promise to cherish him, be faithful to him, and always hold him in highest regard?
Bride: I do.

Minister: Will you uphold these promises to _____ (Groom's Name) today, tomorrow, and for all the days of your life together?
Bride: I do.

★★★

Good Times, Bad Times

Minister: _____ (Groom's Name), do you promise to stay by _____ (Bride's Name) side in sickness and health, in good times and bad, and to tell her when she needs to stop diagnosing herself with rare diseases?
Groom: I do.

Minister: Do you promise to make _____ (Bride's Name) smile when she gets stressed out?
Groom: I do.

Minister: Will you take _____ (Bride's Name) to be your wife, your life partner, your best friend, and will you love, honor and cherish her for as long as you both shall live?
Groom: I do.

★★★

Cherish

Minister: _____, do you give yourself to _____ in marriage?
                    Groom's Name   Bride's Name

Groom: I do.

Minister: Do you promise to encourage her, inspire her, laugh with her, and comfort her in times of sorrow and struggle?
Groom: I do.

Minister: Do you promise to love her in good times and bad, when life seems easy and when it seems hard, when love is simple, and when it is complicated?
Groom: I do.

Minister: Do you promise to cherish her, be faithful to her, and always hold her in highest regard?
Groom: I do.

Minister: Will you uphold these promises to _____ today, and for the remainder of your life together?
                                                                Bride's Name
Groom: I do.

★★★

Love of a Lifetime

Groom: _____, you are my once-in-a-lifetime, my lover, my soul mate, my miracle. You've always brought out the best in me. From your friend, to boyfriend, to fiancé, and your soon-to-be husband, you've helped me grow into the person I am today. Thank you for taking me as I am, loving me, and welcoming me into your heart. I promise to take you as you are – to nurture you, honor you, cherish you, and love you for all time. You are my partner in life. I will remain forever faithful to you, and I will always be here for you, just as you have been here for me. In good times and in bad, I will be alongside you to face any challenge and share in your happiness. When you fall, I will catch you; when you cry, I will comfort you; when you laugh, I will share your joy; and when you press your ice-cold feet against me, goodness knows, they're cold, but I'll still love you. You are my miracle, my love, my spirit animal, my wife.

★★★

You & Me

Minister: _____ , do you promise to love _____
                    Bride's Name   Groom's Name
in good times and bad, when life seems easy and when times are tough, when love is simple, and when it is complicated?
Bride: I do.

Minister: Will you take _____ to be your husband, your life
                                              Groom's Name
partner, and your best friend, and will you love, honor and cherish him for as long as you both shall live?
Bride: I do.

5.9 Ceremony Creation
the ring ceremony

This symbolic act adds context to a part of the ceremony that might otherwise be overlooked. Wedding rings are an important indicator to others that the couple have pledged their lives to each other. By adding a few words, the officiant can weave the exchange into the ceremony, and highlight this important dynamic.

> **in practice...**
> *Ramon grew up listening to tales of how his grandfather romanced his grandmother, back home in Colombia. Growing up, the older man spent hours with Ramon, and a powerful bond developed between the two over the years.*
>
> *When he died, his grandfather left Ramon his wedding ring. And while his grandfather was no longer alive to witness his grandson's wedding, Ramon knew that his grandfather would be proud that he was living life on his own terms. He wanted to wear his grandfather's wedding ring as a symbol of his own commitment to his fiancé, Milton, and so they decided to include a ring exchange ceremony.*

ceremony structure

1. **The Introduction** The officiant explains the significance of wedding rings and the symbolic and real-world implications of the exchange.
2. **The Exchange** The couple exchanges rings while the symbolism of the event is explained aloud. This part works best with the couple repeating after the officiant, since they will be using their hands to exchange rings and the statements are relatively short. Most couples use the same wording for both partners.

Don't forget, the ring exchange has a few moving pieces that you will need to coordinate. In the *Directing the Ceremony* chapter (page 125), we provide a more detailed explanation of the interaction.

examples
the introduction

Direct Connection to the Heart

The wedding ring seals the vows of marriage and represents a promise of everlasting love. It is a physical manifestation of the promises joining this couple together. The wedding ring is placed on the fourth finger of the left hand because years ago, it was believed that this finger was a direct connection to the heart – the perfect place for a symbol representing love and commitment. These rings are the physical embodiment of the spiritual bond that now binds you two together.

✦✦✦

Timeless Symbol

The circle reminded the ancients of eternity, fashioned as it is without a beginning or end; while gold is so incorruptible that it cannot be tarnished by use or time. So may your union, at this time solemnized, be incorruptible in its purity and more lasting than time itself.

✦✦✦

The Whole is Greater than the Sum

Marriage is a state in which two people come together and create a union that is greater than the sum of its parts. As love is so difficult a concept to express in mere words, we use symbols. Since the dawn of humanity, the ring has been an emblem of the sincerity and permanence of a couple's love for one another and the lasting value of their marriage. As the circle can begin anew at any point, so marriage can always be renewed. These rings are symbols of your eternal love.

✦✦✦

Spirit of Love

Now we come to the blessing of the rings. May these rings be blessed as symbols of this affectionate union. These two lives are now joined in one unbroken circle. Wherever they go, they will always return to one another in their unity. These two find in each other the love for which all human beings yearn. They promise to grow in understanding and in compassion. The home which they establish together will be such a place of sanctuary and friendship. These rings, on their fingers, symbolize the Spirit of Love in their hearts.

✦✦✦

Symbol of Marital Union

Through marriage, two people come together and create a union that is greater than the sum of its parts. It is difficult to express in words the profound relationship that is love. The marriage ring is a physical manifestation of the promises joining both the bride and groom together. The wedding ring is placed on the fourth finger of the left hand because it was traditionally believed that this finger was a direct connection to the heart – the perfect place for a symbol representing love and commitment. These rings are visible symbols of your bond.

the exchange

These lines are usually spoken in a "repeat after me" format for both partners.

In My Heart Always

As you, _____ (Partner 1), place this ring on _____ (Partner 2's) finger, please repeat after me: I give you this ring as a symbol of my commitment to you and to our partnership in life. You have my heart always.

✦✦✦

With This Ring, I Thee Wed

As you, _____ (Partner 1), place this ring on _____ (Partner 2's) finger, please

Ceremony Creation the ring ceremony

repeat after me: _____ (Partner 2), with this ring, I thee wed. Wear it as a pledge of my love, and as a symbol of all we share.

✶✶✶

I Promise to You

As you, _____ (Partner 1), place this ring on _____ (Partner 2's) finger, please repeat after me: I promise to you, _____ (Partner 2), before our family and friends, to commit my love to you; to respect your individuality; to be with you through life's changes; and to nurture and strengthen the love between us, as long as we both shall live.

✶✶✶

Honor, Love, & Cherish

As you, _____ (Partner 1), place this ring on _____ (Partner 2's) finger, please repeat after me: I give you this ring as a reminder that I will love, honor, and cherish you, in all times, in all places, and in all ways, forever.

✶✶✶

You Have My Heart Always

As you _____ (Partner 1), place this ring on _____ (Partner 2's) finger, please repeat after me: I give you this ring as a reminder that I will love, honor, and cherish you, in all times and in all places. You have my heart always.

✶✶✶

Surrounded by Love

As you, _____ (Partner 1), place this ring on _____ (Partner 2's) finger, please repeat after me: I give you this ring as a symbol of my commitment to you and to our partnership in life. As it encircles your finger, may it always remind you that you are surrounded by my love.

★★★

This Day and Forevermore

As you, _____ (Partner 1), place this ring on _____ (Partner 2's) finger, please repeat after me: I give you this ring to wear with love and joy. As a ring has no end, neither shall my love for you. I choose you to be my (husband/wife/partner) this day and forevermore. [Then reverse names and title for the other person]

5.10 Ceremony Creation
readings

There are many thought provoking poems and writings that tackle the subjects of love, marriage, friendship, and commitment. While some might associate readings with religious themes, there are just as many secular or agnostic options, and everything in between. In fact, for a couple that wants to avoid religious themes, such readings are the perfect alternative.

No matter what the couple's persuasion, it's always possible to find words that express their feelings for each other. Perhaps it's a song that they learned to love together or a poem that inspires them.

incorporating readings into the ceremony

How and when you present a reading depends on everything else in the ceremony, and how the couple wants it all to flow. Here are some planning suggestions:

Scripture/Religious Readings
It is best to place these readings early in the ceremony. If a devout grandparent or spiritual aunt are expecting acknowledgment of their beliefs, there's no reason to keep them waiting. The sooner you appease the traditionalists, the sooner the ceremony can move on to feature the couple's worldview and relationship. Chances are, you were asked to officiate because the couple wants something other than what their local church had to offer (but that doesn't mean you can't keep traditionally-minded family and friends happy)!

Selecting a Speaker
While the idea of a close friend or relative reading a passage or poem may sound appealing, in practice readings can be tricky to get right. It takes time to transition between speakers, which creates an awkward silence. Further, many people are not great at reading in front of others and don't enjoy public speaking. Make sure your reader has some public speaking

experience, the last thing you want is for someone to choke on stage.

Coordinate
Readings involve additional people that will need to know exactly what they are expected to do, so the actions of the reader should be carefully choreographed. That means thinking out every step, such as having the reader sit close to the front and near the aisle so that they can move into position when it's their time. See *Directing the Ceremony* (page 125), for additional planning tips.

How Many
Keep the readings to a minimum. Two readings usually fit nicely, and we recommend only adding more if you are sure they will fit into the ceremony. If the couple chooses to include multiple *Traditions & Rituals* (page 91), readings fit well in between these additions.

The example readings we have provided are mostly secular and love-focused. For more religious or spiritual passages, see *Religious & Spiritual Words* (page 29). The readings in this chapter are arranged in accordance with where they fit, whether that's early in the ceremony, right before the vows, or as closing readings. That said, our arrangements are only suggestions, and they might work just as well elsewhere in the ceremony.

examples
early ceremony readings

These readings are best placed instead of, or around, the *Words on Marriage* (page 41).

> **What is Love? by Walter Rinder**
> Love is not just looking at each other and saying, "You're wonderful."
> There are times when we are anything but wonderful.
> Love is looking out in the same direction.

It is linking our strength to pull a common load.
It is pushing together towards the far horizons, hand in hand.
Love is knowing that when our strength falters, we can borrow the strength of someone who cares.
Love is a strange awareness that our sorrows will be shared and made lighter by sharing; that joys will be enriched and multiplied by the joy of another.
Love is knowing someone else cares that we are not alone in life.

★★★

Excerpt from *Captain Corelli's Mandolin* by Louis de Bernières
Love is a temporary madness; it erupts like volcanoes and then subsides. And when it subsides you have to make a decision. You have to work out whether your roots have so entwined together that it is inconceivable that you should ever part. Because this is what love is. Love is not breathlessness, it is not excitement, it is not the promulgation of eternal passion. That is just being in love, which any fool can do. Love itself is what is left over when being in love has burned away, and this is both an art and a fortunate accident. Those that truly love have roots that grow towards each other underground, and when all the pretty blossoms have fallen from their branches, they find that they are one tree and not two.

★★★

Marriage Joins Two People in the Circle of Its Love by Edmund O'Neill
Marriage is a commitment to life, the best that two people can find and bring out in each other. It offers opportunities for sharing and growth that no other relationship can equal. It is a physical and an emotional joining that is promised for a lifetime.

Within the circle of its love, marriage encompasses all of life's most important relationships. They are each other's best friend, confidant, lover, teacher, listener, and critic. And there may come times when one partner is heartbroken or ailing, and the love of the other may resemble the tender caring of a parent for a child.

Marriage deepens and enriches every facet of life. Happiness is fuller, memories are fresher, commitment is stronger, even anger is felt more strongly, and passes away more quickly.

Marriage understands and forgives the mistakes life is unable to avoid. It encourages and nurtures new life, new experiences, and new ways of expressing a love that is deeper than life.

When two people pledge their love and care for each other in marriage, they create a spirit unique unto themselves which binds them closer than any spoken or written words. Marriage is a promise, a potential made in the hearts of two people who love each other and takes a lifetime to fulfill.

★★★

Maybe by unknown author
Maybe… we are supposed to meet the wrong people before meeting the right one, so that when we finally meet the right person, we will know how to be grateful for that gift.

Maybe… it is true that we don't know what we have got until we lose it, but it is also true that we don't know what we have been missing until it arrives.

Maybe… the happiest of people don't necessarily have the best of everything; they just make the most of everything that comes along their way.

Maybe… the best kind of love is the kind where you can sit on a sofa together never say a word, and then walk away feeling like it was the best conversation you've ever had.

Maybe… you shouldn't go for looks; they can deceive. Don't go for wealth; even that fades away. Go for someone who makes you smile, because it takes only a smile to make a dark day seem bright.

Maybe… you should hope for enough happiness to make you sweet, enough trials to make you strong, enough sorrow to keep you human, and enough hope to make you happy.

Maybe Love is not about finding the perfect person; it's about learning to see an imperfect person perfectly.

late ceremony readings

These readings are best placed before the closing remarks.

Friendship by Judy Bielicki
It is often said that it is love that makes the world go round. However, without doubt, it is friendship which keeps our spinning existence on an even keel. True friendship provides so many of the essentials for a happy life -- it is the foundation on which to build an enduring relationship, it is the mortar which bonds us together in harmony, and it is the calm, warm protection we sometimes need when the world outside seems cold and chaotic. True friendship holds a mirror to our foibles and failings, without destroying our sense of worthiness. True friendship nurtures our hopes, supports us in our disappointments, and encourages us to grow to our best potential. Today, {Name} and {Name} pledge to each other not only their love, but also the strength, warmth and, most importantly, the fun of true friendship.

★★★

The Art of Marriage by Wilferd Arlan Peterson
Happiness in marriage is not something that just happens.
A good marriage must be created.
In the art of marriage the little things are the big things…
It is never being too old to hold hands.
It is remembering to say "I love you" at least once a day.
It is never going to sleep angry.
It is at no time taking the other for granted; the courtship should not end with the honeymoon, it should continue through all the years.
It is having a mutual sense of values and common objectives.

It is standing together facing the world.
It is forming a circle of love that gathers in the whole family.
It is doing things for each other, not in the attitude of duty or sacrifice, but in the spirit of joy.
It is speaking words of appreciation and demonstrating gratitude in thoughtful ways.
It is not looking for perfection in each other.
It is cultivating flexibility, patience, understanding and a sense of humor.
It is having the capacity to forgive and forget.
It is giving each other an atmosphere in which each can grow.
It is finding room for the things of the spirit.
It is a common search for the good and the beautiful.
It is establishing a relationship in which the independence is equal, dependence is mutual and the obligation is reciprocal.
It is not only marrying the right partner, it is being the right partner.
It is discovering what marriage can be, at its best.

★★★

The Art of Marriage (abridged) by Wilferd Arlan Peterson
 A good marriage must be created.
In the art of marriage the little things are the big things…
It is never being too old to hold hands.
It is remembering to say "I love you" at least once each day.
It is never going to sleep angry.
It is having a mutual sense of values and common objectives.
It is forming a circle of love that gathers in the whole family.
It is speaking words of appreciation and demonstrating gratitude in thoughtful ways.
It is having the capacity to forgive and forget.
It is giving each other an atmosphere in which each can grow.
It is finding room for the things of the spirit.
It is a common search for the good and the beautiful.
It is not only marrying the right partner…
It is being the right partner.

★★★

The Key to Love by unknown author
The key to love is understanding...
as it is the little things that say so much by themselves.
The key to love is forgiveness....
to accept each other's faults and pardon mistakes.
The key to love is sharing...
Sharing and facing your good fortunes as well as the bad, together;
both conquering problems, forever searching for ways
to intensify your happiness.
The key to love is giving...
Giving without thought of return,
but with the hope of just a simple smile,
and by giving in but never giving up.
The key to love is respect...
Respect realizing that you are two separate people, with different ideas;
that you don't belong to each other,
that you belong with each other, and share a mutual bond.
The key to love is inside us all...
It takes time and patience to unlock all the ingredients
that will take you to its threshold;
it is the continual learning process that demands a lot of work...
but the rewards are more than worth the effort...
and that is the key to love.

★★★

On Marriage by unknown author
Treat yourselves and each other with respect, and remind yourselves often of what brought you together. Give the highest priority to the tenderness, gentleness and kindness that your connection deserves. When frustration, difficulty and fear assail your relationship, as they threaten all relationships at one time or another, remember to focus on what is right between you, not only the part which seems wrong. In this way, you can ride out the storms when clouds hide the face of the sun in your lives; remembering that even if you lose sight of it for a moment, the sun is still there. And

if each of you takes responsibility for the quality of your life together, it will be marked by abundance and delight.

★★★

My Love by Linda Lee Elrod
When I met you, I had no idea
how much my life
was about to be changed...
but then, how could I have known?

A love like ours happens
once in a lifetime.
You were a miracle to me,
the one who was everything
I had ever dreamed of,
the one I thought existed
only in my imagination.

And when you came into my life,
I realized that what I
had always thought
was happiness
couldn't compare to the joy
loving you brought me.

You are a part of everything
I think and do and feel,
and with you by my side,
I believe that anything is possible.
(this day) gives me a chance
to thank you for the miracle of you...
you are, and always will be,
the love of my life.

5.11 Ceremony Creation
traditions & rituals

Anyone who has attended a wedding that featured a glass breaking, sand pouring, or ring warming, knows that these rituals can imbue a ceremony with meaning and draw guests into the wedding experience. There's something visceral about uniting the couple through a symbolic act, and couples often want to make their weddings more participatory. Whether it involves guest participation or just the couple, traditions and rituals are a great way to add some diversity to weddings.

> **in practice...**
> As Laura's wedding drew closer she realized that there was little distinction between, "family" and "friends" for her - everyone was "family!" Throughout high school, college, and then in the Peace Corps in Morocco, Laura developed a global network of friends, and many of them were going to be in attendance. With so many close friends showing up, she wanted them to feel included in the ceremony, while also bringing her friends and family closer to her fiancé, Hariesh.
>
> One of our ministers recommended that Laura and Hariesh include a stone blessing ritual in their ceremony, suggesting that guests from around the world could bring small stones from their home countries. The result was a moving experience for all in attendance, and the guests were able to contribute to a physical symbol of the couple's love for each other.

In addition to the stone blessing ritual, there are a variety of traditions that have been used in weddings for generations, and new variations are being added with every wedding that takes place. Older traditions have been adapted to fit modern standards, and some couples are even revisiting ancient rituals.

audience participation

Sand and stone blessing rituals can be a great way to get the audience involved. Stone blessings allow everyone in attendance to contribute a physical endorsement of the couple's union. Sand rituals also provide a sense of collective engagement. By including the children, the sand ritual allows the couple to welcome them into their new family unit.

adding a ritual to the ceremony

There's no "correct" number of rituals to use during a wedding ceremony. It's completely up to the couple. While some choose not to use any ritual components beyond the ring exchange, most couples choose one or two. Ceremonies with many rituals should be structured around them as a series.

If you are aiming for that 20-minute ceremony, it's advisable to stick to one or two traditions or ritual components. Combined with two readings, a family blessing and the personal stories, one or two rituals should close out the ceremony in just under twenty minutes.

examples

The following unity rituals fit well within the ceremony after the ring exchange and before the closing remarks, with the exception of the ring blessing ritual, which must be completed earlier.

Stone Blessing Ritual

_____ and _____, before you met, your lives were on
    Partner 1   Partner 2
different paths with different destinations. But love has brought you together and merged your separate paths into one. Each one of your friends and family here today has a small stone that represents their individuality and presence at your wedding. Each person here has played, or will play, a unique role in your relationship and marriage, which is why you have asked them to be a part of your wedding and this celebration of your love for each other. You also each have a stone of your own that symbolizes your previously separate lives, separate friends, separate families and the different journeys you once traveled.

I now ask that everyone take out the stone you have been given and pause to make a wish or blessing for love and happiness for the couple, for the future of their marriage, or any other wish or blessing you would bestow upon them. Your collective love will empower them as they set out on their journey together, as a married couple.

[Everyone pauses to make their wish]

Now we ask that as you walk out, after the ceremony, please place the stones into the glass vase on the table, and _____ (Partner 1) and _____ (Partner 2) will then add their individual stones to the container as well. This vase will have a special place in their home and will be a beautiful reminder that each of you has joined them today in their celebration of marriage, and of your blessings and good wishes.

As the stones are combined with love into one container, so too are the couple's friends and family joined into one community. Your once solitary life's paths are now one. All that was once separate is now shared, and in this sharing you will find new strength and joy as you set out together on the path of marriage.

Planning
The couple should pick out a bowl or vase that is suitable for display in their home for many years to come. The example above calls for stones, but guests can bring, or be given, glass beads, marbles, shells, wine corks, or anything else that fits their relationship and their home. Before the ceremony, have the stones (or other items) on the welcome table and station someone there to make sure that everyone to takes an item into the ceremony. Alternatively, you can place a stone on each seat. Either way, be sure that you also have three stones close by, for you and the couple to use during the ritual, and make sure that each of the wedding party members have one as well.

During the ritual, while you are saying, "...you each have a stone of your own," you should be taking the stones out of your pocket and allowing the couple to choose from the three you have (the third is for your blessing). Then, allow just a few seconds of silence for guests to make their wishes. It's not meant to be a "bow your head in prayer" type of moment.

Supplies
- One large decorative container to collect the stones.
- Enough stones (or other symbolic objects) for each of the guests to contribute one.

★ ★ ★

Sand Ritual

_____ and _____, today you are making a commitment
    Partner 1   Partner 2
to share the rest of your lives with each other. Your relationship is symbolized by the pouring of these two individual containers of sand; one, representing you, _____, and all that you were, all that you are, and all that you will ever
    Partner 1
be, and the other representing you, _____, and all that you were, all
                                        Partner 2
that you are, and all that you will ever be.

Each one holds its own unique beauty, strength, and character. They can stand on their own and be whole, without requiring anything else. But when the two are blended together they represent an entirely new and extraordinary love. Each grain of sand brings to the mixture a lasting beauty that forever enriches the whole. As you now combine your sand together, your lives also join together as one. Just as these grains of sand can never be separated and poured again into their individual containers, so will your marriage be.

[The couple pours the sand]

> ❗ For couples that want to include their family in the sand ritual, this is a great way to welcome them into the collective family unit. If younger children are involved, we recommend that they pour with the couple, however, have the couple start pouring first, given the symbolic significance of their actions. If younger children are involved in this component, you can add the following words:

94 | **Ceremony Creation** traditions & rituals

> You are joined together today, not only in marriage, but as family. Just as these grains of sand can never be separated and poured again into their individual containers, so will your marriage and family be.

And if the children are older, the couple should pour their sand first, and then add:

> _____ – _____ and _____ love you
> Children's Names   Partner 1   Partner 2
> very much, and want you to know that you are, and will always be, a very important part of their lives. Will you please pour some sand into this glass container along with your good wishes?"

Planning

The couple will need to buy a sand ritual kit, or assemble their own. For the latter, they will need; one larger container and two smaller containers and two different colors (or types) of sand.

Before the ceremony, make sure that the two smaller containers are filled with the sand, and that those containers, as well as the larger receptacle, are all on a table behind or next to you. The table on which the sand ritual is set up should be situated so that the couple can walk behind it. Their positioning will allow everyone to watch as they pour their individual containers of sand into the larger one.

Tip – The larger container should have a wide opening, and if not, make sure to provide a funnel.

Supplies

- Sand, in two different types or colors.
- Containers: two smaller containers for the different sands, and one larger container into which the sand will be poured during the ritual.
- Funnel, (if the larger container doesn't have a wide mouth).

✦✦✦

Wine Ritual

For thousands of years, wine has been used to celebrate special occasions, and today is certainly such an occasion! _____ and _____, will soon
_{Partner 1}   _{Partner 2}
be sharing a glass of wine. As most of us know, wine is both bitter and sweet, with the different flavors combining in a way that makes each wine unique. Life will have its bitter moments and its sweet moments, unique to this couple. Just as you share from this glass of wine together, you will share moments in life together – some sweeter, and some more bitter. But ultimately, because you are doing it together, the sweet moments will be sweeter, and the bitter moments less bitter.

Please now share this glass of wine. The sweetness of it is our wish for your married life!

Planning

All this ritual requires is a single glass, some wine (we recommend white wine, so that if it's knocked or spilled, the damage is minimal), and a small table or ledge where you can put the glass. When you say, "please now share this glass of wine," hand the glass to the first partner and once they take a sip, pass the glass to the other to take a sip. Once they have both drunk, return the glass to the table/ledge.

Supplies

- Wine glass
- Wine, preferably white

✦✦✦

Rose Ritual

Your gift to each other on your wedding today has been your wedding rings – which shall always be an outward demonstration of your vows of love and respect, and a public showing of your commitment to each other. Now, for your first gift as husband and wife, you will also give each other the gift of a single rose.

For thousands of years, the rose has been a symbol of love. The rose says, simply, "I love you." And so, it is appropriate that your first gift as (husband and wife/partners/spouses) is a single rose.

_____ (Partner 1) and _____ (Partner 2), please exchange your roses.

The roses that you now hold, both given and received, represent the most precious gift in this life – one I hope you always remember – the gift of true and abiding love within the devotion of marriage.

_____ (Partner 1) and _____ (Partner 2), I would ask that wherever you make your home, you pick a special place for these roses; so that on each anniversary of your wedding, you may take a rose to that same place, both as a recommitment to your marriage, and as a recommitment that this will be a marriage based upon love.

_____ (Partner 1) and _____ (Partner 2), in the years ahead, never forget that that it was love that brought you here today. Never forget that only love can make your marriage a glorious union, and always remember that only through love can your marriage endure.

Planning

All that is needed for this ritual are two roses (to make it easy, ask the florist to add two roses to the order). They can be kept behind or near the officiant until it is time for the exchange: right before the line, "... _____ (Partner 1) and _____ (Partner 2), exchange roses." At the end of the ritual, you can take roses back from the couple, so that they don't have to hold them for the rest of the ceremony.

Supplies

- Two roses

✦✦✦

Hands Blessing Ritual

[The couple should already be holding hands, as this is intended to immediately follow the *Ring Ceremony* (page 77)]

As you hold hands here today, please enjoy and appreciate the gift that these hands are to you. These are the hands of your best friend. Full of love, you hold your partner's hands on this wedding day, as you promise to love each other today, tomorrow, and forever. These are the hands that will work alongside yours, as together you build your future. These are the hands that will passionately love you and cherish you through the years, and with the slightest touch, comfort you like no other. These are the hands that will hold you when fear or grief fills your heart. These are the hands that will wipe the tears from your eye, whether they be tears of sorrow, or tears of joy. These are the hands that will tenderly hold your children. These are the hands that will help you hold your family as one. These are the hands that will give you strength when you need it. And lastly, these are the hands that, even when wrinkled and aged, will still be reaching for yours with that same unspoken tenderness.

Planning

Nothing to worry about here at all – they should already be holding hands, and that's all you need to commence this ritual.

If this is the only ritual that you are including in the ceremony, it fits well immediately following the *Ring Ceremony* (page 77). The Hands Blessing can also be moved to before the *Vows* (page 57), just remember to remind the couple to hold hands.

Supplies

- None!

★★★

Ring Warming Ritual

To all of you in attendance, your presence here is not only important to the couple, it's also an honor for them to have you here. As such, _____ and _____ request that each of you individually share in their ceremony.
_{Partner 1}   _{Partner 2}

[Hold up the rings in an organza bag or other small pouch.]

I hold here the rings that _____ and _____ will exchange to symbolize their love, but before that, they have asked that all of you warm them with your blessing. As the rings are passed between those of you at this gathering, please pause for a moment, and while holding their rings, offer a silent prayer, blessing, or wish for _____ and _____ in their new life together. Wish them love and happiness, wish that their hopes and dreams for a life together will become a reality, or wish for them whatever is in your heart. Your loving energy will help to move and carry them on the journey that they will share as a married couple.

This gesture will allow _____ and _____ to feel all of the love and tenderness that you are carrying for them in your hearts. They will wear these rings every day of their lives knowing they are truly infused with the love and blessings of their dearest ones.

[Pass the bag with the rings to someone nearby to get the process started – the Maid of Honor is a great place to start.]

> ❗ We recommend that you begin this ritual after the *Opening Remarks* (page 25). It is smart to include this ritual early on, as the rings need time to move through the assembled guests. This ritual works best at smaller weddings, because even if it only takes a few seconds for each guest to bless the rings, the collective blessings quickly add up.

Planning

You will want to have the rings in a small container, either before the ceremony, or after the ring bearer brings them. Start with the maid of honor or another wedding party member, and have them instruct the next person in the row to pass it along.

The idea is that the bag or box containing the rings works its way through all of the guests, starting on one side, and ending up on the other, like an extended game of "telephone."

The last member of the wedding party to bless the rings will then hold the bag until you are ready for it. Don't forget to give the couple a chance to add their own wishes to the rings, and make sure to add yours before you take the rings out of the container for the exchange.

Supplies
- The Rings!
- Small container for the rings, a small organza bag or box.

5.12 Ceremony Creation
closing remarks

It's finally time to wrap it up! As the emcee of the ceremony, it's your job to bring the ceremony to a nice, tidy conclusion. While there are plenty of ways to deliver these final words, make an effort to be concise and retain the tone of the ceremony through to the end, with an emphasis on love and commitment.

> **in practice…**
> *With the reception scheduled to start just minutes after the ceremony was to conclude, Jaka and Merle wanted to end on a high note! The ceremony they had planned was rather formal, so they wanted to remind their guests how excited they were to be starting their married life together.*
>
> *Working with their officiant, the couple were careful not to undercut the formality of the event, while also pointing their guests to the bright future that lay ahead. Beginning with a reminder that they would stick together through their "joys, and their sorrows," and "console each other in their times of need," the closing remarks then pivoted towards a lighthearted reminder that they would always be there to laugh at each others jokes, and be each other's best friend.*

Aim for about a paragraph in length with your closing remarks. At this point, you're in the home stretch and you don't want to bore the guests.

examples

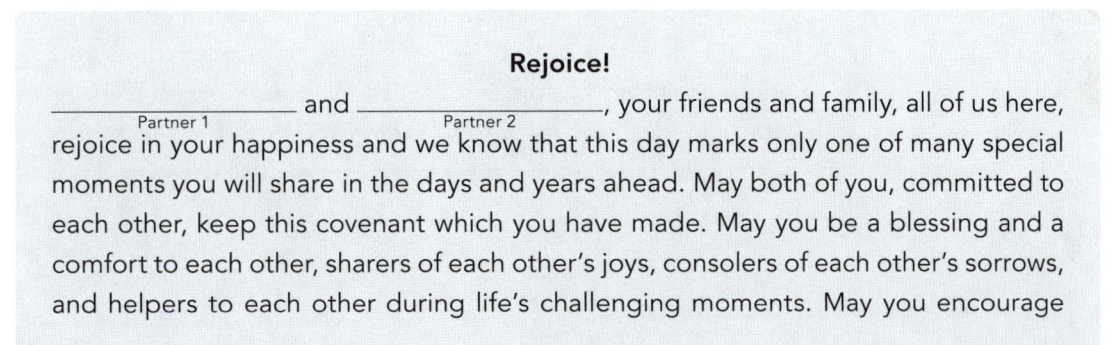

Rejoice!
_____ (Partner 1) and _____ (Partner 2), your friends and family, all of us here, rejoice in your happiness and we know that this day marks only one of many special moments you will share in the days and years ahead. May both of you, committed to each other, keep this covenant which you have made. May you be a blessing and a comfort to each other, sharers of each other's joys, consolers of each other's sorrows, and helpers to each other during life's challenging moments. May you encourage

each other in whatever you set out to achieve. May both of you, trusting each other, go forth fearlessly. May you not only express and accept affection between yourselves, but also reach out with love to all people. We hope that the inspiration of this hour will not be forgotten. May you continue to love and cherish one another forever. And may you always find reasons to laugh, both with, and at, each other!

★★★

New Beginnings!

As this ceremony nears its end, the marriage of _____ (Partner 1) and _____ (Partner 2) nears its beginning. This union, as we can plainly see, will be filled with love, joy, and laughter. The progression of this amazing relationship has brought them to this special day during which they publicly vowed to be partners for life. I know I speak for everyone here when I say that we are honored to have been chosen to witness those vows.

As _____ (Partner 1) and _____ (Partner 2) enter into marriage, we wish them a lifetime of happiness and all want to convey our love for, and to them, right from this beginning.

★★★

To a Wonderful Marriage!

Looking at the love _____ (Partner 1) and _____ (Partner 2) have for each other and hearing the vows they made to each other, I can only conclude that this will be a wonderful marriage. A marriage that will surmount the bad times and thrive in the good times. A marriage in which both of you will grow and succeed, as you support each other in your current and future endeavors. We are honored to have been here today at the start, and we look forward to seeing you both ten years from now, when you will be a bit older, maybe a bit wiser but definitely still the incredible couple we see before us today.

★★★

Lifelong Partnership

The commitment you two have made to each other today is deeper than the vows that you made. It is a personal commitment to a lifelong partnership. It is an agreement based on the trust that you both will support and nurture each other with the same intensity in 10, 20 or even 50 years from now. And, the love you two have shown for each other today is deeper than any of the readings or other words shared. It is a love that will allow the relationship to thrive through good times and bad. It is a love that will be a part of everything you do as individuals and as the wonderful couple we see before us today.

⭐ ⭐ ⭐

Gamblers

Gamblers talk about something called risk-versus-reward. The theory is that you should evaluate the odds and not risk more than you could get in return. Is marriage a risk? Most of us would answer yes to that question. But knowing that, you two nonetheless took that risk and vowed to be partners for life. Now, it's clear to everyone here that you both bet on a winning hand. But, I also want to remind you to let this risk be your guide to making the best choices as your relationship develops. There are times when the relationship will require you to fold, there are times when the relationship will require you to pass, and then there are times when the relationship will require you to go all in. And if you're in doubt about how to play your hand, listen to your hearts.

⭐ ⭐ ⭐

Savor the Moment

Having just heard the wonderful vows you made to each other, I want to pass on a few words of wisdom to remember in the times ahead. As the pomp and circumstance of this wonderful wedding fades and life returns to normal, remember what you have promised to each other, in not only words, but also with the actions that led up to this marriage. It's clear to us all that the words, actions, and accompanying thoughts that led you two to this moment were of love for each other and commitment to each other. And trust me when I say that both of these will be tested as you navigate married life together. There will be great times, but there also will be not-so-great times, and it is during the not-so-great times that you need to remember this day, and all the wonderful reasons why you got married.

★ ★ ★

Stronger as a Pair
We are almost there; you have just sworn your love to each other, and promised to support and remain committed to each other. In just a moment, I will make the pronouncement that everyone has been waiting to hear. But before we do that, and while I still have everyone's attention, I want to wish you, _____ (Partner 1) and you, _____ (Partner 2) a wonderful life together and remind you to never take the other for granted. As you settle into married life together, remember that you are stronger as a pair than as individuals. You will make mistakes. We all do. But the key is to remember the reasons why you are together, why you got married, and why you love the other person. Remember these reasons, communicate with each other, have a good laugh or cry, and as long as you do so together, you will be able to get through anything.

5.13 Ceremony Creation
pronouncement, kiss, & introduction

It's now time for the thrilling conclusion of the ceremony!

The pronouncement, kiss, and introduction of the newlyweds are three unique pieces, however, they happen in such rapid succession, that we have chosen to group them together. It shouldn't take you long to write these parts of the ceremony, but it is crucial that you get the details right. Here especially, the couple's values, and perhaps even their politics are important considerations.

identity

When planning, a good place to start is by asking the couple whether they will be changing their last names, merging them, or keeping their own? Do they want to be referred to as "spouses," or " husband and wife," or some other designation? As the officiant, you don't want to be introducing Mrs. Black as Mrs. Wilson if she's chosen to retain her maiden name. The best way to avoid this sort of confusion is to communicate, so make sure that's happening.

> **in practice...**
> *Asneth and Shireen both worked in academia, and both had publications under their maiden names. While they liked the idea of sharing a last name, they realized that doing so might jeopardize their future prospects, so they decided to stick with their respective family names, in this case Waverly and Nassir.*

Couples might choose to retain their family names for any number of reasons, or choose a combination, such as "Waverly-Nassir" (see example below). As long as the officiant and the couple are on the same page, the pronouncement will carry the same gravity and significance as the traditional "Mr. and Mrs. Smith."

This will be the couple's first introduction to the world as a married couple, so it's important to get it right. Consider running through the wording with the couple a few times, so they get a chance to hear what it sounds like.

the pronouncement

The officiant has significant leeway when it comes to scripting this part of the ceremony, and many first time officiants like to have some fun with this section ("by the power vested in me by the internet..."). While short, the pronouncement is crucial to the ceremony, as it confers official, and social recognition upon the union.

the kiss

Much like the *Parent's Blessing* (page 21), many couples are happy to learn that they have options when it comes to the wording of this seemingly-small part of the ceremony. For some, the more traditional "you may now kiss the bride" is what they want to hear, while others prefer something more modern or egalitarian. There are a lot of variations to this part of the ceremony, so feel free to adapt it to suit the couple.

For example, one couple chose to word it as follows: "Shannon, you may now kiss your bride, and Kelly, you may now kiss your groom!" Another same-sex couple chose the following variation: "You may now each kiss the groom." As always, there's no right or wrong way to phrase this part, as long as it's clear what's happening to the couple and audience.

the presentation/introduction

This is the very last piece in the ceremony, and it's crucial that it reflects how the couple wants to introduce themselves to the world. Many couples look forward to hearing "Mr. and Mrs." or some variation thereof for the first time, but not everyone will feel this way. Some might want another option for their introduction, while others will choose to omit this part altogether, ending the ceremony with the kiss.

Don't assume that the couple have chosen the "Mr. and Mrs. Smith" model when you make your pronouncement. It is just as common for the couple to retain their last names, or combine the two. Ask the couple, and make sure they have reviewed the final draft of this part of the ceremony.

examples
the pronouncement

By the Book
Now that you have spoken the words and performed the rites that unite your lives, I do hereby, in accordance with your beliefs and the laws of _____ (Name of State), declare your marriage to be valid and binding, and I declare you, _____ (Partner 1) and _____ (Partner 2), to be (husband and wife/spouses/a married couple or other chosen designation).

✦✦✦

It's Official!
_____ (Partner 1) and _____ (Partner 2), you are now officially, as you already have been in your hearts, (husband and wife/spouses/a married couple or other chosen designation).

✦✦✦

An Honor
It is my honor and privilege to now pronounce you Legally Married Partners.

✦✦✦

With Great Joy
Having witnessed your marriage vows, along with all who are assembled here today and by the authority vested in me by the State of _____ (State Name), it is with great joy that I now pronounce you united and legally married, spouses for life.

✦✦✦

Expressions of Love

_____ and _____, you have showered our hearts with
 Partner 1   Partner 2
expressions of your love, and promised each other the joy of all your days. Before these witnesses, it gives me great honor and pleasure to pronounce you (husband and wife/spouses/a married couple, or other chosen designation).

✦✦✦

Together in Marriage

You have declared before all of us that you will live together in marriage. You have made life-long promises to each other, through your vows and the exchange of wedding rings. Having pledged yourselves each to the other, I do now, pronounce you to be (husband and wife/spouses/a married couple or other chosen designation).

the kiss

You may now kiss your bride/spouse!

✦✦✦

You may now seal your vows and promises with a kiss!

✦✦✦

You may now seal your commitment with a kiss!

✦✦✦

You may now celebrate your marriage with a kiss!

★★★

You may now celebrate with your first kiss as husband and wife!

★★★

We will now finish the ceremony and begin your marriage with a kiss!

presentation/introduction

It is my incredible honor to introduce for the very first time as a married couple, **Asneth Waverly** and **Shireen Nassir**! (Or can be Mr. and Mrs. Smith, or Mr. and Mr. / Mrs. and Mrs. Smith)

★★★

It is my honor to introduce the newlyweds, _____ and _____!
                                              Partner 1   Partner 2

★★★

Please join me in celebrating _____ and _____!
                                Partner 1   Partner 2

★★★

I am honored to present, for the very first time, _____ and
                                                   Partner 1's First Name
_____! (For example "Steve and Rachel Ross" or "Jill
Partner 2's First Name and Their Chosen Family Name
and Abby Blair-Smith")

★★★

At the starting of the ceremony, you joined me in welcoming them by their individual names; now join me in celebrating them as the married couple Mr. and Mrs. _____.
　　　　　　Chosen Last Name

5.14 Ceremony Creation
ceremony assembly

Congratulations, you've made it through the ceremony creation part of *Asked to Officiate*, and you can now fit the pieces together to make the perfect wedding ceremony. Just think about it like a play or movie script, but unlike Shakespeare who had to start from scratch, we've given you a pretty good cheat sheet.

Five Critical Components

Let's briefly review the five critical components of a wedding ceremony.

1. Opening Remarks
2. Vows
3. Ring Exchange
4. Closing Words
5. The Pronouncement, Kiss, and Introduction

Take a few minutes to sketch out some ideas for these parts, decide which of our examples you want to use, and voilà, you'll have the framework of your ceremony! If you need to jog your memory, you can always refer back to *Ceremony Creation: An Introduction* (page 17). And if you've already had your *Planning with the Couple* (page 13) meeting, you'll have a pretty good idea of any additional parts that need to be worked in.

If you've still got questions, we've got answers. Visit the *theamm.org* to see how other AMM Ministers have innovated.

6 Preparation for Ceremony Delivery

At this point, you should be quite far along in preparing the ceremony, if not already finished. That means the big day is drawing closer and you will soon be officiating the ceremony in front of the couple, their friends, and their families. You've invested a lot of time into getting the ceremony right, so don't skimp on the delivery!

If you are a certified Toastmaster or have extensive public speaking skills, you can skip this chapter. If not, keep reading.

Since you said "yes" to officiating, we know you're up to the task, but you probably still need some pointers. This chapter won't turn you into a motivational speaker overnight, but we do have a few tricks to help you knock this ceremony out of the park!

the basics

The first thing that any experienced public speaker will tell you is to *know your material, backwards and forwards*. The more you practice, the better your delivery will be. Those well spoken politicians, celebrities, and business leaders you see on television - they have practiced for hours! Most people's fear of public speaking stems from their fear of forgetting, or scrambling their lines. A few extra runs through the material is often enough to eliminate the jitters. If you're still nervous, give the script a few more reads. Eventually, it will become second nature.

Practice, practice, practice. And when practicing, don't just read the ceremony to yourself, you want to read it out loud. Try reading in front of a mirror a couple times. After you're familiar with the script and flow, read the ceremony to a friend who can provide constructive criticism. Building on your friend's suggestions, run through the ceremony a few more times. Remember, the more you practice, the more confident you'll be during the real deal.

consider both words and actions

As you practice, take notes. These notes can be as simple as reminding yourself to pause at a certain point, or underlining a word or phrase that you want to emphasize.

While practicing, time how long it takes you to complete the ceremony. If friends or family of the couple will be participating in the ceremony, make sure to account for the time it will take them to assume their places and read their lines. You may even want to grab a couple of friends and have them stand in to read the lines that will be spoken by friends and family.

managing your nerves

By using the tips above, you'll know the ceremony inside and out. That way, even if you are still nervous, you'll do a great job. And speaking of nervousness, even AMM Ministers who have conducted hundreds of ceremonies still get the jitters when it's time to go on stage. Why? Because every single ceremony is important, and like you, we are invested in creating a once-in-a-lifetime experience. For most officiants, being nervous is part of the job, but you have the tools to overcome it – just practice!

We've seen our share of weddings, as well as our share of creative ways to manage stage fright. From the best man who has a couple of shots to "loosen up" to the nervous officiant chain smoking out back, we've seen it all! And while the booze may be flowing – it's a wedding after all – we don't recommend alcoholic beverages, since they can quickly lead to slurred speech and other side effects. It's easier to stay sober and in control.

When your time comes to step in front of the room, clear your mind and take a few deep breaths. Remind yourself to take it slow, and remember to smile, and project confidence.

engage with the audience

When you start speaking, try to do more than simply "read the ceremony." One of the reasons that you practiced so many times was so that you could look up periodically and engage the audience. This allows you to truly "speak" to the couple and guests. Make eye contact, allow for a few dramatic pauses. It's fine to take a few seconds in between paragraphs to collect your thoughts.

Finally, remember that you are doing this to honor the couple, and in presenting the ceremony, you get to be an integral part of their special day. With the right preparation, you will enjoy the officiating experience. Once you get into the swing of things, you can embrace the joy and wonder of love and marriage, and then amplify it. The couple and everyone else in attendance will pick up on your enthusiasm, and respond accordingly.

> I've learned that people will forget what you said, people will forget what you did, but people will never forget how you made them feel.
> — Maya Angelou

7 Rehearsing the Ceremony

The ceremony script is finished, edited, and agreed upon by everyone involved at this point; you've also spent plenty of time practicing. You aren't just satisfied with your work, you're proud of it! Now, it's time for us to pivot to the next part of this book, executing your carefully planned ceremony. The following chapter covers the steps involved in rehearsing the wedding. During this phase, there are bound to be minor complications, botched lines, and other unexpected occurrences but don't let that phase you. If someone forgets their lines or finds themselves in the wrong place at the wrong time, just make a note of it and help them get it right during the second, or third take. By being friendly and helpful, we're confident that you'll get the best performance possible out of the wedding party.

working with a wedding planner

Is a professional wedding planner involved? If so, your job just got a lot easier. Even if there isn't a wedding planner, many wedding venues will have an event coordinator on hand. Either way, let them handle the rehearsal. These folk have lots of experience running rehearsals. And since they will be the ones doing the final line-up on the wedding day and sending people down the aisle, they should also be running the show during the rehearsal.

If there is a wedding planner or venue coordinator, make sure to tell them what pieces are being included in the ceremony, since that dictates how they manage the rehearsal, and of course, the wedding itself. Make sure the wedding planner knows if a *Parent's Blessing* (page 21) will be asked, and how the ceremony will end. Does it end with the kiss, or will you be presenting the couple as the closing act?

If a wedding planner or event coordinator is running the show, your only involvement during the rehearsal, besides practicing your role as officiant of course, will be if there are *Traditions & Rituals* (page 91) included in the ceremony. In that case, your task is to familiarize the couple with where they need to stand, and what they need to do. In the upcoming *Directing the Ceremony* chapter (page 125), we'll go into more detail about how the officiant guides the couple through the ceremony as it happens, but the more they know in advance, the better. That will allow you to focus on your delivery, rather than stage managing the couple.

no planner, no problem

You've just found out that there's no wedding planner or event coordinator and everyone is counting on you, the officiant, to execute the rehearsal and ceremony. If that's the case, don't worry, we've got you covered!

Your primary objective is to familiarize the wedding party with the ceremony space and establish everyone's roles and actions. Simply put, the rehearsal is where the officiant and wedding party practice walking in, where you designate how everyone stands and what they do, and then practice walking out. The rehearsal is not for practicing the ceremony, since you want it to be a surprise for everyone on the wedding day.

Remember what you are trying to accomplish:

1. The wedding party must understand what to do and where to go during the ceremony.
2. The wedding party must know when to arrive before the ceremony, for getting ready and pictures.
3. Any children involved should get a bit of practice walking down the aisle, sprinkling flower petals or carrying the ring pillow.
4. The marriage license must be accounted for. Make sure you have the marriage license on hand, or designate a person who understands its importance responsible for bringing it to the ceremony.

Every-single-member of the wedding party (the couple, the officiant, the wedding party, attendants, flower children, ring bearers, readers, and other family members taking part in the processional and recessional) should meet at the ceremony site and "run through" the walking in, standing, and walking out. If the ceremony site is unavailable for the rehearsal, find a space where you can simulate the setup/conditions.

By the time the ceremony rehearsal is over, everyone will know exactly when they should walk in and out, who will be walking ahead of and behind them, who will be walking with them, and any cues the officiant might be using to direct people during the ceremony. Running through all of this is especially important when there is a large wedding party or if children are participating.

Traditional weddings featuring a bride and groom tend to have more defined roles and customs than weddings featuring same-sex couples, who have a lot more flexibility. The following guidance therefore features the designations "bride and groom," however in most cases, those titles are interchangeable with "partner one and partner two."

ok, so you're running the rehearsal

Remember, this process is designed to get everyone familiarized with their role in the ceremony, so don't worry about mistakes. That's why you're rehearsing!

Ideally, the couple will have already decided the order in which their attendants will line up, enter and exit, and where they would like them to stand, walk, or sit. Encourage the couple to take a leadership role. If everyone is pulling their weight, there is no reason for a rehearsal to last longer than one hour.

step one – get your ducks in a row

A. Line up the wedding party where they will be standing during the ceremony. The traditional wedding formation has the groom and his attendants on the officiant's left, and the bride and her attendants on the officiant's right. Same sex couples can choose who stands where, but regardless of the couple, it's just a matter of of personal preference.

B. The couple faces each other, holding hands.

C. (Optional) The ring bearer should be in front of the groom's attendants, or sitting with the parents or grandparents.

D. (Optional) Flower children should be in front of the bride's attendants, or sitting with the parents or grandparents.

step two – practice the recessional

A. After the officiant has pronounced the couple married, they kiss, and are presented as newlyweds.

B. The couple exits.

C. The attendants and officiant wait until they get all the way down the aisle, to allow the photographer to take pictures of the couple walking up aisle.

D. If any flower children or ring bearers are standing, they exit next.

E. Attendants from each side meet in the center and walk out as couples. The best man and maid of honor are first. Generally, it's best for one pair of attendants to make it halfway up the aisle before the next pair starts walking.

F. The bride's parents exit.

G. The groom's parents exit.

H. The bride's grandparents exit (if they have mobility issues, it's fine for them to stay seated).

I. The groom's grandparents exit (again, if they have mobility issues, it's also fine for them to stay seated).

J. The officiant exits - this is then the signal that the guests can get up and walk out.

step three – now, start from the top

If the couple has recruited ushers, they will seat the family and guests of honor, who are not part of the official processional. The front row should be reserved for these individuals. At the rehearsal you can practice escorting in these guests. Remind them to wait in the back for their escort.

Here's the suggested order of entry for special guests that are not in the procession:

1. Grandparents of the groom
2. Grandparents of the bride
3. Parents of the groom
4. Mother of the bride

step four – the processional

We could write an entire book on this - there are as many ways to do the procession as there are weddings. We've seen couples escort each other in, dance down the aisles, and everything in between. The three most common processions are slightly staider, but they've stood the test of time. All three start after the seating of the grandparents and/or the parents:

Option One The groom and his attendants enter from the side of the room or space, heading right to the front, while the bride and her attendants enter from the back and go down the aisle.

Option Two The groom enters with the officiant (this could be from the side or down the aisle), while the attendants come down the aisle in pairs.

Option Three The officiant enters from the side or is first down the aisle. The groom escorts his mother and/or his soon-to-be mother in law down the aisle, while the attendants come down the aisle in pairs.

lead up to and entry of the bride

The wedding party enters and stands in their designated spots. The first attendants to walk in should be those standing farthest from the couple, filling in one pair at a time, until finally the maid of honor and best man, standing closest to the couple, enter as the last pair.

A. The ring bearer enters and either sits with someone (if he or she is young) or stands in front of the attendants. It may be hard for a young child to stand up front for the entirety of the ceremony, so it's advisable that he or she returns to the audience once the handoff has happened.

B. The flower children (sometimes accompanied by the ring bearer) enter and then sit with their parents after spreading petals up to the altar.

C. As the bride prepares to enter, the officiant motions for the guests to rise, or says, "please stand."

D. The bride begins making her way down the aisle, with her escort.

E. As the bride approaches the front, the groom may take several steps forward and offer the bride his arm or hand (the groom is on the bride's right).

> **!** If the escort is going to answer the Parent's Blessing, he or she can answer the question while standing at the front of the room with the bride. Only after the question is asked and answered, does the groom take the bride's hand or arm. The two of them then approach the officiant, leaving the escort standing next to the row in which he or she will be seated – usually on the bride's side.

what about the kids?

There's a good chance that the flower children and ring bearers will need assistance as they make their way down the aisle. We've all seen it. They might become distracted, confused, or throw a tantrum, and that's perfectly fine as long as their parents are close by and able to step in. This means that the parents should sit near the aisle, with easy access to the action.

That's not to say that a little childlike spontaneity can't make for some classic wedding moments, but you've been asked to officiate, not babysit.

Consider using fake rings for the ring bearer. This way, if he or she drops the rings or decides that they want to keep them – they are after all very shiny and pretty – it won't disrupt the ceremony, or precipitate a crying fit during the ceremony.

step five – practice

You now have everyone back up on stage in their spots.

- Run through the ceremony, paying attention movement

- Familiarize any family or guests coming up to read with when they will be invited up, and where they should stand.

- Let's talk about the kiss. Sure, the couple are just hours from their wedding, but kissing in front of an audience is a whole different kettle of fish.

- Close out the practice by presenting the couple as you will during the actual ceremony and then practice having the couple can walk out followed by their attendants.

you made it!

Congratulations, you made it through the ceremony rehearsal! Now do it again. Seriously, you want the event to go off without a hitch and with so many moving parts, there's plenty of room for error. If the wedding party mastered the ceremony during the first run through, the second take will be short and sweet. That way, you and the couple can rest easy going into the big day knowing that the ceremony will go smoothly.

You've just accomplished the heavy lifting, and deserve a pat on the back! Did the attendants initially stand in the wrong spot? Did Great Aunt Margaret approach the stage too early for her reading? Those glitches don't matter anymore because you've got them out of the way now. Thanks to your efforts, the wedding is going to go off without a hitch, creating beautiful and lasting memories.

8 Directing the Ceremony

It's the big day, and whether you like it or not, once you're up there in front of the guests, you are in charge of the ceremony. Standing, sitting, flowers, rings, microphones, vows – there's a lot going on in that 15-20 minute window, which is why we've provided a list of pointers and reminders help you keep track.

please stand

This tradition is pretty standard, to the point where rising for the bride is taken for granted. Nonetheless, it doesn't hurt to clarify what's expected. What if there are two brides, or the couple are less traditional?

At this point, most of us are so conditioned by the movies and television shows we've grown up with that rising is habitual. A simple "please rise for the bride," will suffice, and folks will jump to their feet. As the officiant, you'll be facing the entrance, so it's your responsibility to ask the guests to rise when you see her enter the room.

You may also want to coordinate this part of the ceremony with the DJ or musicians, as the bride's entrance is often accompanied by a change in music.

For LGBTQ weddings, as discussed in *LGBTQ Couples* (page 7), there are a variety of options for the entrance and procession, so don't make any assumptions. Some same-sex couples will want the guests to rise for both entrances while others would rather the guests stayed seated, so make sure you accommodate these wishes.

the parent's blessing

While we covered this topic extensively in the *Parent's Blessing* chapter (page 21), it's worth revisiting from the logistics perspective. For this part of the ceremony, the bride and her father (or parents) come to a stop at the first row of chairs where the family are sitting, and answer the question facing the groom and officiant.

Directing the Ceremony | 125

After the question, the waiting groom/partner approaches the bride and shakes the escort's hand (or hugs), then the couple join hands and takes the final few steps to their designated positions in front of the officiant. By taking the final few steps together, the couple are "coming to marriage as equals and as a choice" rather than the bride being "brought to marriage."

please be seated

Give the guests permission to be seated while the hugging and/or shaking of hands is happening between the couple and escort. This takes place either after the parent's blessing or when the couple are making their way towards the officiant. This way, the guests are seated and able to watch the couple take the final steps towards the officiant. A simple, "please be seated" is all you need to say.

the flower handoff

Once the couple is in front of you, quietly remind the bride to hand her bouquet to the Maid of Honor. That way she will have both hands free to hold hands with the person she is marrying.

how to stand

While there are a variety of ways to stand during the ceremony, one simple solution is for the couple to stand in front of the officiant, facing each other holding hands. This allows them to see and connect with each other, while also letting their families and friends to see their faces, at least in profile, during the ceremony.

> ❗ The couple might need to be quietly reminded to hold hands at this point, and at subsequent moments during the ceremony.

where to sit

While the "bride's side" is traditionally on the left and the groom's is on the right, consider reversing that for the immediate family members in the front row or rows. Thus, the groom's parents would sit on the same side of the room as the bride stands (or partner one's family on the same side as partner two).

126 | **Directing the Ceremony**

This will allow them to look across and see their family member's face as they get married, and not just the back of their dress/suit.

vows

If the couple decide to say their vows using either the "I do" or the "repeat after me" variety, then all you need to do is have your own copy of the script.

If the couple chooses to read their own vows, it's a good idea to print their respective scripts and affix them to a note card. Use a font that's readable from a distance; you don't want the couple squinting at tiny text. When it's time for the vows, simply hand the correct cards to each partner and take them back when they are finished.

We mentioned this earlier, but it's worth reiterating: while there is no set order of who reads their vows first, we recommend that the "bigger crier" goes first, as they might have a harder time getting through their own vows after they've just heard their partner's vows.

After you've taken the cards back, you might need to remind the couple to hold hands again.

tissues

It's not a wedding without some crying. The emotional intensity of such moments can catch even the most impassive people off guard, prompting a few tears. Be at the ready with tissues, the couple will appreciate it.

rings

We recommend giving the best man both of the rings, as the Maid of Honor usually has her hands full holding flowers. It's also best to remove the rings from their boxes/cases beforehand. That way you will avoid the awkward struggle of removing the rings when the time comes to hand them off. This also keeps the unsightly "ring box bulge" out of wedding photos.

Remind the best man to have the rings at the ready at a predetermined point in the ceremony, usually after the vows, when the subject matter turns to rings. ==At that point, reach your hand behind the groom, and the best man will put both rings in your hand==. That way you can hand the proper ring to each person when it's time.

Who puts their ring on first is entirely up to the couple. Just be sure to discuss this in advance, and make a note of it if you're worried you'll forget.

the readers

Ideally before the rehearsal, and certainly before the ceremony itself, talk to the friends and family who will be reading, and explain when they should ready themselves and make their way to the front. Make sure that you have established whether or not the reader will be bringing the text themselves, or if you are responsible for it. Some readers prefer to have a copy of their excerpt well in advance, so that they can practice reading it and familiarize themselves with the text. Regardless of who is bringing the text, it's a good idea to print the words on note cards, in a large and readable font.

> A great way to introduce a text and the reader is by saying something along the lines of, "We now invite Martha's Aunt Judy who will be reading to us from, the *"Art of Marriage."*

traditions or optional components

If the couple has chosen to include any traditions or optional components, it's likely that you will need to still guide them through the steps – remember, they will likely be anxious and nervous up there, so some subtle guidance will go a long way.

For example, during the sand ritual, when it is time for them to go over to the table, you should back out of the way and gesture for them to walk behind the table. Once the ritual is finished, you can gesture for them to return to standing in front of you, and hold hands again.

microphones

When it comes to technology, you're at the mercy of whatever setup the ceremony musicians or DJ bring. Nonetheless, it's a good idea to familiarize yourself with the possibilities. The following are common options for microphones: a lavalier microphone clipped onto your shirt or dress, a microphone on a stand, or a hand-held microphone.

Clip-On Lavalier Microphones

These are the best option, and the easiest to use. These microphones pick up your voice well, and won't stand out in the pictures. The only drawback is that, during the couple's vows, you may need to unclip the microphone to hold it closer to the couple, so that it picks up their voices. Alternatively, the DJ might have a second microphone which he or she can hand you, allowing you to keep the lavaliere on. In that case, have the handheld microphone somewhere nearby, and reach for it when it's time for the vows, either holding it in front of them, or letting them hold it.

Microphone on a Stand

The second best option is a microphone on a stand, situated between you and the couple. If the microphone is sensitive enough, it can be lowered so that it doesn't show up as prominently in photos. If it is not as sensitive, and therefore needs to be pointed at you during the ceremony, you will need to turn the microphone to face the couple during their vows.

Handheld Microphone

The third common option is a handheld microphone, which can be awkward. With one hand always occupied holding the microphone, it becomes harder to engage in other parts of the ceremony such as handing off the rings or handing the couple their vows. And even if you're especially dexterous, it gets tiring holding a microphone up to your face for extended periods of time. If the clip-on option is not available, arrange for a stand; it will make officiating much easier.

the kiss

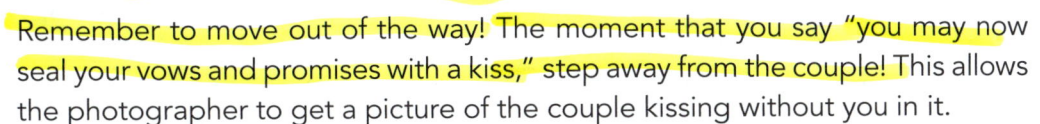

Remember to move out of the way! The moment that you say "you may now seal your vows and promises with a kiss," step away from the couple! This allows the photographer to get a picture of the couple kissing without you in it.

Directing the Ceremony | 129

returning the bride's flowers

After the couple has kissed, remind them to turn and face the guests while holding hands. With her free hand, the bride should then receive her flowers from the Maid of Honor. This allows her to have that beautiful bouquet in the pictures as they are walking back down the aisle.

post ceremony announcements

Since you still have the microphone after the couple has left the front of the room, this is a perfect opportunity to inform the guests about the reception, and any other subsequent events or details to be aware of. Check with the couple or the wedding planner (if there is one), about what to say.

The most common way to make these announcements is to say something along the lines of, "if we could ask that the immediate family stays behind for pictures, _____ and _____ invite the
                          Partner 1   Partner 2
rest of you to enjoy cocktails at the _____."
                                              Location

Alternatively, the DJ might be the one tasked with making the announcements, but it's worth checking.

ceremony delivery format

Technology has made officiating a lot easier. In the past, the officiant had two options – memorize, or write the script down and read from cards or a sheet of paper. With tablets, it's much easier to import the ceremony from your computer. This option is increasingly popular, however some couples might not want your tablet in their wedding photos, which means you're back to doing it the old fashioned way.

> **Note Cards**
> Once you have a finalized draft of the ceremony, and added your notes, change the margins of the document to 0.75" on all four sides and make the text large enough to be readable. Then, print it, cut it out, and glue it to the cards. This might seem like a lot of work, but you don't want to be wrestling with a floppy sheet of paper, especially if the wedding is outside

and there's a breeze.

Tablet
While this option is convenient, the screen might be hard to read if you are standing in the sun, even with a glare protector. If you choose this option, make sure that your battery is full and that the text is formatted to be readable during the ceremony.

Once the ceremony is finalized and you have added your notes, save the ceremony as a PDF. Now you can easily scroll through the ceremony as you go.

Binder
Many officiants use a black binder, which you can find in any office supply store. If the wedding is outside, buy the plastic slide-in binder pockets or sheets to avoid problems with the wind.

dressing the part

You can ask the couple if they have any preference regarding what you wear, but a good rule of thumb is, "dress neutral." You don't want your clothes clashing with the couple's choice of color or their level of dress. It's best to err on the side of caution and dress modestly. Don't over-dress, and don't under-dress. One outfit that works well is a black or gray suit with a white shirt; or just black or gray slacks, a white shirt, and no jacket. If you want to wear a dress, consider using similar tones, in a more formal style. Remember, your choice of outfit as an officiant is likely to be different from what you would wear if you were attending the wedding as a guest.

If in doubt, visit *theamm.org* and scroll through the thousands of pictures that our officiants have uploaded to get some ideas.

the marriage license

We've made it to the final item on the checklist, and you're almost ready to go! Since you are most likely officiating a legal wedding, rather than a commitment ceremony or renewal of vows, there will be some paperwork to take care of afterwards.

The couple will need to pick up a marriage license before the wedding day, which is then completed after the ceremony. It will generally come with instructions, and as the officiant, your role is to sign and return that license to the office where it was issued.

Marriage license regulations vary by state, and sometimes county or municipality. Remind the couple to apply with their local office early!

Getting the marriage license squared away is a priority. The ceremony will soon devolve into celebration and socializing, and with every minute that passes, it's going to be harder to gather the requisite signatories. We advise that you communicate all of this to the couple, required witnesses (traditionally the maid of honor and best man), and the photographer before the ceremony, so that you can all agree on where you are headed after the ceremony. This allows you to take care of this critical legal component before the couple and their families head off for pictures, the reception, and whatever else is on the schedule.

When everyone else has signed the document, all that's still required is your signature, and perhaps some information that you'll need to fill in. Find a quiet spot where you can take your time completing the license. Some states or counties or towns are picky about how marriage license are filled in, so be careful and double check your work. For more details about how to complete this task, make sure to check out *theamm.org*

9 Delivering the Ceremony

it's showtime!

You did your research. You created a ceremony that fits the couple. You practiced that ceremony. The preparation is done, and now it's go time.

enjoy!

First and foremost, enjoy the experience! Everyone in attendance, including the couple, will pick up on your energy and enjoyment of this important moment. Smile, breathe deeply, don't rush, and enjoy the ride!

final thoughts on delivery

You have two audiences – the couple that you are helping to unite, and the families and friends who are there to celebrate with the couple. At times, you will be talking to the couple, and at times you will talking to the entire room. No matter who the immediate audience is, make an effort to draw everyone in and make them feel like they are part of the experience. Eye contact is a powerful tool. As you progress through the ceremony, switch between looking at the couple to looking past them at the faces in the audience. Pick out a friend or acquaintance somewhere in the crowd, and engage with them every so often.

You want to put the couple at ease, which means that you have to be in control. Your comfort level is key to making the couple feel at ease. If folks are still nervous, humor will dispel their anxiety. Remind the couple to "take a deep breath," while breathing in deeply yourself. That usually breaks the tension. Remind the couple to look around at everyone who has come to celebrate with them, and pause while they do so. The guests will enjoy this as much as the couple does. This simple activity will build a sense of camaraderie that further dispels any anxiety.

our closing wish

It is our sincerest wish that our accumulated experience, presented here in *Asked to Officiate* makes your officiating a meaningful, enjoyable, and memorable experience. From all of us at American Marriage Ministries, and from the hundreds of thousands of ministers that have gone before you, we wish you the best of luck!

And finally, on behalf of the couple and the community that you are serving with your efforts, we thank you for being a force of positivity as you unite couples, bring communities closer, and celebrate the beauty and joy of marriage.

Glossary of Frequently Used Terms at AMM

Officiate

To **Officiate** is to perform a service or ceremony, like a marriage!

Letter of Good Standing

A **Letter of Good Standing** is a letter affirming your status as a minister. At AMM, we issue **Letters of Good Standing** to provide additional proof of your credentials, as is required for **Registration** in some states.

Marriage Certificate (commemorative)

A commemorative **Marriage Certificate** is a great keepsake, and we offer many designs through the AMM store. It is meant for gift-giving or display only, and should not be confused with the **Marriage License** - which is the couple's official document of marriage.

Marriage License

A **Marriage License** is the official document of marriage that is recognized by the government. A couple must obtain a **Marriage License** from their local county clerk/recorder, allowing them to get married in that state (and/or county). This is what the **Minister** will complete after performing the ceremony.

Minister

A **Minister** is someone authorized by a church or religious organization to perform services or ceremonies. AMM Ministers are ordained based upon the honorable intent of the individual in pursuance of the AMM's principles, to perform marriages for friends, family, and those in their community.

Officiant

When it comes to marriage, the term **Officiant** describes someone who has authorization from their local government to perform a ceremony and sign the couple's **Marriage License**. In most states, an AMM Ministers is automatically an **Officiant** - in fact, judges, elected officials, notaries, and even ship captains are recognized as **Officiants** in some states.

It is important to do your research. Some states require **Ministers** to **Register** with the government, to become authorized as **Officiants**.

Ordained / Ordination

To be **Ordained** is to have title or status granted by a church or religious organization – AMM Ministers are recognized as ministers, and they have been granted that title by American Marriage Ministries. **Ordination** is the process of receiving that title or status.

Ordination Certificate

An **Ordination Certificate** is an official record of one's **Ordination** with a church or religious organization.

At AMM, an official **Ordination Certificate** is affixed with AMM's seal, and accepted by government offices as proof of ordination. As an AMM Minister, you may order a copy of your *Ordination Certificate* online: theamm.org/store

The unofficial, digital copy of your **Ordination Certificate** is available online to save or print for your own personal record keeping, however the digital version is not accepted as proof of your ordination by government offices.

Processional

At the start of the ceremony, the **Processional** is the formal entrance of the wedding party, ending with the entrance of the bride in traditional weddings.

Pronouncement

The **Pronouncement** is the **Officiant's** public declaration that the couple are now married, commonly phrased, "I now pronounce you…"

Recessional

At the end of the ceremony, the **Recessional** is the formal exit of the wedding party. The newly married couple usually exits first, followed by the rest of the wedding party.

Registration

At AMM, we use the term **Registration** to refer to the process of individual ministers registering with a government office, prior to performing a ceremony. Some states require ministers to do this - and those policies vary from state to state - so be sure to verify whether or not you have any additional steps to take after getting ordained: theamm.org/minister-registration

Solemnize

To **Solemnize**, in the context of marriage, is to make officially perform a marriage. This is the role that the **Officiant** plays. Most jurisdictions in the United States require solemnization for a marriage to be legally valid.

Vow Renewal

A **Vow Renewal** ceremony, or renewal of vows, is a celebratory ceremony, where an already married couple reaffirms their commitment to each other. From the government's perspective, a **Vow Renewal** is purely ceremonial and does not require a **Marriage License** or **Registration** for the **Minister**.